Jilly Austwick

MOTIF MAGIC

for hand and machine knits

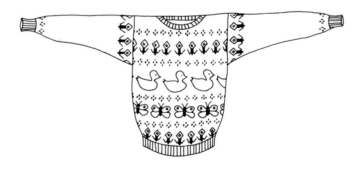

A DAVID & CHARLES CRAFT BOOK

ABBREVIATIONS . . .

. . . for hand knitters

Alt	alternate
Beg	beginning
Cm	centimetre
Dec	decrease
Foll	following
gm	gram
Inc	increase
Inc 1	work into the front and back of stitch
K	knit
Tog	together
K2 tog	knit two stitches together
P	purl
Rem	remaining
Rep	repeat
Rep from *	repeat all the instructions that follow *
St	stitch
St St	stocking stitch

. . . for machine knitters

NWP	non-working position
WP	working position
UWP	upper working position
HP	holding position
N	needles
L	left
R	right
Carr	carriage
St(s)	stitch(es)
in	inches
cm	centimetres
MY	main yarn

WY	waste yarn
R(s)	row(s)
T	tension
K	knit
MT	main tension
FI	Fair Isle
beg	beginning
EON	every other needle
RC	row counter
Alt	alternate

CONVERSION CHART
(centimetres to inches (approximate))

cm	inches	cm	inches
1	0.5	21	8.25
2	0.75	22	8.75
3	1.25	23	9.0
4	1.5	24	9.5
5	2.0	25	10
6	2.25	26	10.25
7	2.75	27	10.75
8	3.25	28	11.0
9	3.5	29	11.5
10	4.0	30	11.75
11	4.25	31	12.25
12	4.75	32	12.5
13	5.0	33	13
14	5.5	34	13.5
15	6.0	35	13.75
16	6.25	36	14.25
17	6.75	37	14.5
18	7.0	38	15
19	7.5	39	15.25
20	7.75	40	15.75

British Library Cataloguing in Publication Data
Austwick, Jilly
  Motif magic: for hand and machine knits.
  1. Knitting. Motifs
  I. Title
  746.43'2

  ISBN 0-7153-9426-6

Distributed in the United States of America by
Sterling Publishing Co. Inc,
387 Park Avenue South, New York, NY 10016

Typeset in Goudy by ABM Typographics Ltd Hull
and printed in Italy by New Interlitho SpA
for David & Charles Publishers plc
Brunel House   Newton Abbot   Devon

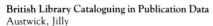

CONTENTS

INTRODUCTION

Both hand and machine knitting are currently enjoying a return in popularity. Each year, many books are published on the subject, appealing to the traditional hand knitter or to the new machine-knitting enthusiast. Given an understanding of the basic techniques, this book can be used by anyone. Whether you use the latest electronic machine or prefer to stick to knitting needles, these designs will provide an endless source of inspiration to knitters of any standard. You will be encouraged to use your own ideas and create garments which are fun to make and fashionable to wear.

Throughout the course of history Man has expressed himself by the use of visual images and symbols. His clothes have always reflected his status and personality. In fact, the word 'knitting' derives from an Old English word meaning 'a knot'. Methods have varied slightly over the centuries and are subject to regional variation, but in essence the basic techniques have remained the same throughout the 3000 years that knitting is known to have existed. Today's knitted garments are not only practical and hard wearing, but provide a visual means of showing individuality by use of colour, texture and pattern.

All of the patterns in this book can be used with a variety of yarns, from mohair to double knitting. This means that you can knit the same pattern in two different materials and achieve a totally different effect. Basic knitting techniques are used throughout and all of the motifs can be worked by using stocking stitch, a stitch familiar to both hand and machine knitters.

The key to successful knitting lies in the tension. If the tension is not correct, if it is too tight or too loose, then no matter how good the pattern is, you will be disappointed. Most commercially produced patterns rely on a combination of the wool thickness, the size of the needle and the stitch combination.

Left: Border and repeat pattern jumpers (pages 122 & 126)

When you begin to knit, you have to learn a new language. It is essential to be able to read the pattern at a glance. Very often, this is far from easy until you have gained years of experience. Even seasoned knitters find some patterns far from easy. In this book I have attempted to do away with lengthy, detailed instructions. The aim has been to make the patterns simple, easy to read and hence, quick to knit. How many jumpers have ended up in the knitting basket to be 'finished one day, when I get round to it'?

As you study the book, you will find that the instructions have been conveyed in chart form, based on simple basic shapes. The whole idea is to let the knitter enjoy creating the motifs. Once you are familiar with their design, you can apply the Teddy Bear, or the Seal, or the Duck, or whatever catches your eye, to your own favourite knitting pattern. Whether you are a machine knitter, or a hand knitter, there is something in this book for you. All you need is some imagination, some wool and a little bit of time, and you can create garments that are unique to you, your family and your friends.

USING THIS BOOK

You will find this book extremely easy to use if you follow some simple guidelines. After all, the whole idea is to start knitting, not to spend time working out the patterns; that has all been done for you. First of all, it is important to remember that each square on the chart represents a single stitch – whatever method of knitting you choose to use.

① **Decide on the method of knitting** This is easy. Choose either hand or machine.

② **Choose the pattern, the size and the yarn** Not so easy as you have quite a choice.

③ **Knit a tension swatch** Having decided on how you are going to knit the garment and how big it will be, chosen the pattern and selected the yarn, you must then knit a tension swatch. This must be matched as closely as possible to the tension recommended in this book. The patterns have been worked on an average tension for each different type of yarn.

④ **Decide on the motif** Now you can really make a start. Before you start knitting though, make sure that there are sufficient rows in your garment to knit the length of your chosen motif.

YARNS

The variety of wools, cottons, acrylics and other man-made fibres available today has little in common with ancient yarns, but their purpose remains unchanged. To make the most of the huge range of yarns currently available to the hand and machine knitter, a basic knowledge of the various types is essential. Yarn is actually a continuous single strand of natural or man-made fibres, twisted together. Each single strand is known as a 'ply'. All yarns have a ply classification, but the reference to the ply does not necessarily determine the thickness of the finished yarn. The plys can be thick or thin depending on the types of yarn which are twisted together.

Hand-knitting yarns fall into various groups according to how they are constructed:

2-, 3- and 4-ply Classic yarn for general use.

Double knitting Hard wearing and very popular for hand knitting as it knits up quickly.

Aran One and a half times the thickness of Double Knitting.

Chunky or Double-double Knit Twice the thickness of Double Knitting.

The choice of yarn for each pattern must be yours.

NATURAL FIBRES

Natural fibres fall into two main categories, either animal or vegetable. Wool from sheep is the most common animal fibre. However it varies enormously in length, quality and strength. Each of these attributes are affected by local conditions –

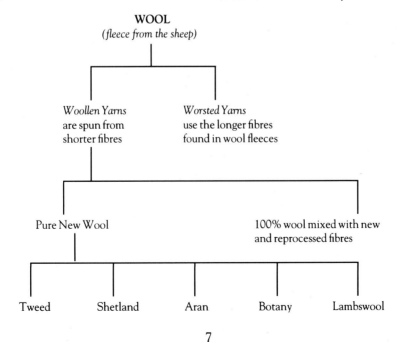

WOOL
(fleece from the sheep)

Woollen Yarns
are spun from
shorter fibres

Worsted Yarns
use the longer fibres
found in wool fleeces

Pure New Wool

100% wool mixed with new
and reprocessed fibres

Tweed   Shetland   Aran   Botany   Lambswool

This page: Maxwell Mouse (page 47) and Squatting Frog (page 64). Right: Border and repeat pattern jumpers (pages 122 & 126)

where does the sheep come from? What is it grazed on? There are one thousand million sheep in the world, with by far the largest populations in the southern hemisphere. Cross breeding and the development of individual species to produce specific fibre properties have rewarded the knitter with a wide range of versatile and durable yarns. The natural crimping of the wool fibre means that after stretching, the wool will return to its natural position, a major contributory factor to the continued popularity of woollen yarns.

Aran Aran is a traditional style of knitting which used 4-ply wool. It originates from the island off the Irish coast whose sheep produced a thick rough fibre with a natural creamy colour. The wool is warm, strong and very hard wearing. The name is now applied to any yarn of similar appearance whether naturally occurring or man made, either the traditional off white or brightly coloured.

Botany A very fine wool which is now mainly produced in Australia. Lambswool comes from the first shearing of Merino lambs. It is extremely fine and is very soft.

Shetland The original Shetland wool was spun from the soft wool of the Shetland Island sheep. Today, the term is applied to any wool which has the same characteristics, including man-made fibres.

Tweed A thick wool made of strong, coarse fibres. It usually has coloured specks spun into the yarn.

HAIR
Fibres from the coats of animals other than sheep are generally described as hair. These naturally occurring fibres include Mohair, Angora and Cashmere.

Mohair Mohair is derived from the Angora goat. It is very warm and light, hard wearing and distinctively thick and fluffy.

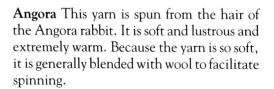

Angora This yarn is spun from the hair of the Angora rabbit. It is soft and lustrous and extremely warm. Because the yarn is so soft, it is generally blended with wool to facilitate spinning.

Cashmere A wonderfully soft, smooth and light yarn which comes from the Kashmir goats of Northern India.

VEGETABLE FIBRES

Cotton The most common vegetable fibre derives from the cotton plant found throughout the world. Cotton yarns are available in many colours. They are versatile, hard wearing and are distinguished by their ease of washing.

MAN-MADE FIBRES

Modern science and technology have given knitters access to a wide range of man-made fibres. Often they are much cheaper than natural fibres. They combine light weight with bulk, and wash extremely well, even in a washing machine. The marriage of wool and synthetic fibres results in the best features of both being combined to give a soft woollen texture with the strength and washability of the man-made fibre.

The main raw materials for synthetic fibres are wood, coal and oil. Their derivatives are Nylon, Polyester and Acrylic.

Nylon This was the first synthetic fibre to be developed and successfully marketed for use in yarns. It is usually combined with wool.

Polyester Similar to nylon for its strength and durability, it is particularly noted for its drip-dry qualities. It is usually blended with wool.

Acrylic This yarn is not as strong or hard wearing as nylon or polyester, but its feel is much closer to wool than the other synthetics, hence its popularity.

TEXTURED YARNS

This group of yarns is almost all based on synthetics, though they are usually mixed with other natural fibres. Aran, Mohair, Angora and many other natural yarns now have synthetic equivalents. On the whole, the synthetic yarns tend to be much cheaper than the real thing. However, they are excellent for picture or motif knitting as their wide range of textures and colour variations can bring out the full beauty of the design.

Bouclé This yarn gives an uneven, knobbly finish to the garment.
Brushed yarn The fibres of this material have been brought out to produce a fluffy effect.
Chennile Produces a smooth, velvety feel.
Crêpe A very smooth yarn which has been twisted to produce a characteristic crinkle.
Loop A garment knitted with this yarn has built-in loops. Great care must be taken not to catch the loops with the knitting needles.
Slub As the name implies, this yarn produces a fine fabric, with occasional lumps, resulting in a unique texture.

COLOUR AND OTHER ENHANCEMENTS

The effect that colour can have on a garment is magical. Simply by changing one key colour, a totally different mood can be created. Using bright primary colours a design can be made to jump out at you. Yet the same design, knitted in soft pastel shades, gives a feeling of lightness and subtlety. A change of texture from, say, Double Knitting to Mohair, can add further dimensions. Mixing of yarns and textures can emphasise a motif, perhaps by making it stand out in relief.

Of course any of the designs can be further enhanced by embroidery. Small details can be added to give an extra dimension in terms of colour and texture. The most commonly employed technique is Swiss darning, which imitates knitting and results in a slightly raised stitch, perfect for eyes, noses, buttons and many other small, but important, details. Try adding tassels, pompons, appliqué and buttons to your sweater and let your imagination run riot.

BUYING YOUR YARN

Wools and other yarns can be purchased by the ball, by the cone, or in a hank or skein, but they are all sold by weight. Wool for hand knitting is generally sold by the ball; for machine knitting, by the cone. Yarns sold by the skein tend to be of a very thick nature and must be wound into a ball before use, or on to a cone if you are using a machine. This is very easily achieved using a wool winder.

The only real restriction that you will find when you go out to buy the yarn is its thickness. Hand-knitting yarns usually come as 3- or 4-ply, or Double Knitting. This is not an indication of weight or thickness, merely an indication of the number of individual strands that make up that particular yarn. For machine knitters, yarns are available in specific thicknesses to match the different-size needles on the various machines.

YARN LABELLING

The ball band around a ball of wool is full of useful and essential information. It usually tells you:

a) What the fibre content is
b) Where it was made
c) The quantity of yarn
d) The washing instructions
e) The needle size (for hand knitters)
f) The shade number and dye lot (batch). *

Machine-knitting yarns tend not to have this information so readily displayed. If you need help, ask at your specialist wool shop.

*Wool is dyed in batches and as such, there may be slight variations in colour between each batch. It is usually only slight, but it can make the difference between a perfect garment and one with a funny-coloured band around it, because that part was knitted with wool from a different batch. The only sure way to avoid this possibility is to overestimate slightly when buying your yarn. This avoids the chance of the wool shop selling out of that particular batch of yarn when you are halfway through your sweater.

Approximate Quantities of Yarn (gm)				
Size	4-ply	DK	Mohair	Aran
18	100	150	–	–
20	125	175	–	–
22	150	200	–	–
24	200	250	–	–
26	225	300	–	–
28	275	325	–	–
30	300	350	–	–
32	350	400	–	–
S	400	450	450	650
M	450	500	500	700
L	500	550	550	750
XL	550	600	600	800

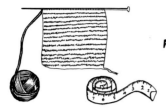

TENSION

Having chosen the yarn and pattern, the time has come to knit a tension square. This small, but nevertheless important, piece of knitting is vital to the successful working of the patterns in this book because no particular manufacturers' yarn has been recommended. Tension varies between knitters. The same piece of knitting made by three different knitters will result in three different tensions, so it is of the utmost importance to work a tension square, not only to check the tension, but to give you a more accurate estimate of the amount of yarn required to make the garment.

FOR HAND KNITTERS

There are three factors which affect the tension of a piece of hand knitting.

a) The size of needles and type of yarn.
b) The type of stitch. (NB All the patterns are in stocking stitch.)
c) The individual knitter.

To knit a tension square, choose your yarn and follow the chart below. This will give you the approximate tension you require to hand knit a garment from the patterns in this book. The finished piece of knitting should measure 10cm (4in) square.

Yarn	Needle size	Stitches	Rows
DK	4mm (8)	22	28
Mohair	5mm (6)	18	22
Aran	5mm (6)	18	24

Remember that thicker yarn requires a slacker control and that thinner yarns need a much tighter control.

If, when measuring your finished tension square, you find that it is too loose, try using a smaller needle. Conversely, if it is too tight, then use larger needles.

FOR MACHINE KNITTERS

The tension will vary depending on the machine that you are using. Therefore you must knit up a tension square with the yarn that you propose to use, according to the instructions given in your manual. The chart below sets out the approximate tension dial settings that you will need to follow the patterns in this book. The finished tension square measurement is 10cm (4in) square.

Yarn	Tension dial setting	Stitches	Rows
4-ply	6	30	40
Chunky	4	18	22

The tension dial may need to be adjusted if the knitting is too slack or too tight.

Most machine-knitting yarns have been waxed or oiled so that they go through the machine without snagging. When using these yarns, you must wash the finished tension square before measuring it. One word of warning – never press an acrylic tension square. It makes a mess on the iron and it doesn't do much for the knitting either.

Pig on the Wall (page 67), Elephant (page 98) and Clown (page 97)

MACHINE-KNITTING METHODS

Before you start, read the manual for your machine from cover to cover. There is nothing more frustrating than to reach a point in a pattern, stop and consult the manual, and then find out that you should have done something three rows back and that really you should start again.

Patterning techniques tend to differ and it is very important to know the capabilities of one's machine. The first sixty graphs are designed to be knitted by the Intarsia Method (Method 1). However, if you will be using only one contrasting colour, then they can be knitted on an electronic machine (Method 2). Some of the scattered motifs and border repeat patterns can be knitted on any machine with a 24-stitch patterning facility.

When machine knitting, do not forget that the wrong side of the work faces you as it comes out of the machine, so that the motif is actually reversed on the right side.

METHOD 1 (INTARSIA)

Intarsia sounds very technical, but in fact it is simply a term used to describe picture knitting. There is no limit to the number of colours that can be knitted in one row other than your own ability to cope with a myriad of different colours.

The technique simply involves laying the different coloured yarns over the needles when you come to a colour change. The carriage will automatically knit the yarn and then line up the needles for the next rows. Do not forget to cross the yarns when you change colour, otherwise you will be left with holes around the edge of the motif.

METHOD 2 (ELECTRONIC MYLAR)

Most electronic machines will knit a 60-stitch pattern drawn on a Mylar sheet, though some of the newer electronic machines have a memory. As the owners of these machines will already know, their great advantage is their ability to change the position or size of the motifs automatically. Unfortunately, automatic patterning on a knitting machine limits the user to just two colours in any one row.

METHOD 3 (PUNCHCARD/24-STITCH PATTERNING)

Provided the cards are punched correctly on the recommended card for your machine, the patterns will work on any automatic 24-stitch machines. Do not forget however, that a punchcard will limit you to only two colours per row.

METHOD 4 (CHUNKY MACHINE)

The basic techniques of Intarsia knitting apply whether you are using a Chunky or a standard gauge machine. Some Chunky machines have a 24-stitch facility.

Whichever method you choose to use, machine knitting operates at considerable speed; problems may occur if the yarn is unprepared. Most machine-knitting yarns are treated to allow a free flow of wool through the machine. Untreated yarns can lead to jams and dropped stitches. To overcome this, some machines have a wax disc on the aerial tension unit. If your machine does not have this facility, then the answer is to simply spray the yarn with a specially prepared knitting silicone.

BASIC SHAPES AND PATTERNS

BASIC PATTERNS

Hand knits

Double-knit round neck	17
Double-knit slash neck	20
Mohair round neck	22
Mohair slash neck	24
Aran round neck	25
Aran slash neck	27

Machine knits

Standard gauge 4-ply round neck	30
Standard gauge 4-ply slash neck	33
Round neck jumper for chunky machines	35
Slash neck jumper for chunky machines	38

Dropped shoulder, round neck.

Dropped shoulder, slash neck.

All the garments are designed to be loose and baggy. If you need a more fitted style, then knit a size smaller.

Teddy Bear and Duck (page 50)

DOUBLE-KNIT ROUND NECK

Use 3.25mm (10) needles for ribs and 4mm (8) needles for stocking stitch.
A tension square must be knitted - the correct tension should be
22 stitches and 28 rows to 10cm (4")

TO FIT		CHILDREN				ADULTS			
SIZES	cm	66	71	76	81				
	"	26	28	30	32	S	M	L	XL
FINISHED SIZE	cm	72	78	83	88	94	102	110	117
	"	28.5	31	32.5	34.5	37	40	43	46
SLEEVE LENGTH	cm	36	41	43	46	56	56	56	56
	"	14	16	17	18	22	22	22	22
FINISHED BACK LENGTH	cm	41	48	52	56	69	69	69	69
	"	16	19	20.5	22	27	27	27	27
BACK Using 3.25mm needles, cast on		81 sts	87 sts	93 sts	99 sts	91 sts	101 sts	111 sts	121 sts
Work in K1 P1 rib		22 rows	22 rows	22 rows	22 rows	28 rows	28 rows	28 rows	28 rows
increasing in the last row *		-	-	-	-	16 sts	16 sts	16 sts	16 sts
Change to 4mm needles and work in stocking stitch (standard)		116 rows	128 rows	140 rows	152 rows	156 rows	156 rows	156 rows	156 rows
Change to 4mm needles and work in stocking stitch (longer)						184 rows	184 rows	184 rows	184 rows
SHOULDER SHAPINGS Cast off at the beginning of the next		11 sts	12 sts	13 sts	15 sts	11 sts	13 sts	14 sts	16 sts
		4 rows	2 rows	2 rows	4 rows	4 rows	4 rows	6 rows	4 rows
Cast off at the beginning of the next		-	13 sts	14 sts	-	10 sts	11 sts	-	15 sts
		-	2 rows	2 rows	-	2 rows	2 rows	-	2 rows
Leave remaining on a spare needle		37 sts	37 sts	39 sts	39 sts	43 sts	43 sts	43 sts	43 sts

DOUBLE-KNIT ROUND NECK contd

FRONT Knit as for back to *								
Change to 4mm needles and work in stocking stitch (standard)	102 rows	114 rows	126 rows	138 rows	136 rows	136 rows	136 rows	136 rows
Change to 4mm needles and work in stocking stitch (longer)					164 rows	164 rows	164 rows	164 rows
TO SHAPE NECK Knit	32 sts	35 sts	37 sts	40 sts	44 sts	49 sts	54 sts	59 sts
K2 together, turn P2 together								
Working on these stitches, decrease 1 stitch at the neck edge on the next	10 rows	10 rows	10 rows	10 rows	12 rows	12 rows	12 rows	12 rows
Now work in stocking stitch	2 rows	2 rows	2 rows	2 rows	6 rows	6 rows	6 rows	6 rows
At beginning of the next row, cast off	11 sts	12 sts	13 sts	15 sts	11 sts	13 sts	14 sts	16 sts
ADULTS ONLY Work one row, then cast off					11 sts	13 sts	14 sts	16 sts
Work one row, then cast off the remaining	11 sts	13 sts	14 sts	15 sts	10 sts	11 sts	14 sts	15 sts
Slip the next on to a spare needle	13 sts	13 sts	15 sts	15 sts	15 sts	15 sts	15 sts	15 sts
Re-join the yarn to the next stitch and work second side to match the first, reversing all shapings.								
SLEEVES Using 3.25mm needles, cast on	47 sts	49 sts	51 sts	53 sts	55 sts	55 sts	55 sts	55 sts

DOUBLE-KNIT ROUND NECK contd

Work in K1 P1 rib	22 rows	22 rows	22 rows	22 rows	28 rows	28 rows	28 rows	28 rows
Change to 4mm needles and work in stocking stitch, increasing 1 stitch at each end of the next and every 4th row to	79 sts	85 sts	91 sts	97 sts	111 sts	111 sts	111 sts	111 sts
Continue without shaping until sleeve measures	34cm	38cm	42cm	46cm	52cm	52cm	52cm	52cm
	13.5"	15"	16.5"	18"	20.5"	20.5"	20.5"	20.5"
Cast off loosely								
NECKBAND Join right shoulder seam. using 3.25mm needles and with the right side facing you, pick up and knit along left side of neck	18 sts	18 sts	18 sts	18 sts	19 sts	19 sts	19 sts	19 sts
From centre front	13 sts	13 sts	15 sts	15 sts	15 sts	15 sts	15 sts	15 sts
From right side neck	19 sts	19 sts	19 sts	19 sts	20 sts	20 sts	20 sts	20 sts
From back neck	37 sts	37 sts	39 sts	39 sts	43 sts	43 sts	43 sts	43 sts
Work in K1 P1 rib	5 rows	5 rows	5 rows	5 rows	7 rows	7 rows	7 rows	7 rows
Cast off loosely in rib								
TO MAKE UP Join left shoulder. measure down from shoulder seams	18cm	19cm	20.5cm	22cm	25cm	25cm	25cm	25cm
	7"	7.5"	8.25"	9"	9.75"	9.75"	9.75"	9.75"
Place markers on the side seams								

Back stitch sleeves into position between the front and back markers.
Sew up side and sleeve seams using back or ladder stitch.

DOUBLE-KNIT SLASH NECK

Use 3.25mm (10) needles for ribs and 4mm (8) needles for stocking stitch.
A tension square must be knitted - the correct tension should be 22 stitches and 28 rows to 10cm (4")

TO FIT		TODDLERS				CHILDREN				ADULTS			
SIZES cm		46	51	56	61	66	71	76	81				
"		18	20	22	24	26	28	30	32	S	M	L	XL
FINISHED SIZE cm		53	58	63	68	74	79	84	89	98	107	116	125
"		20.5	22.5	24.5	26.5	29	31	33	35	38.5	42	45.5	49
SLEEVE LENGTH cm		21	24	27	30	34	38	42	46	52	52	52	52
"		8.25	9.25	10.5	11.75	13.5	15	16.5	18	20.5	20.5	20.5	20.5
FINISHED BACK cm LENGTH (standard)		30	34	38	42	48	52	56	60	64	64	64	64
"		12	13.5	15	16.5	19	20.5	22	23.5	25	25	25	25
FINISHED BACK cm LENGTH (longer)		-	-	-	-	-	-	-	-	74	74	74	74
"		-	-	-	-	-	-	-	-	29	29	29	29
BACK & FRONT(ALIKE) Using 3.25mm needles, cast on		57 sts	63 sts	69 sts	75 sts	81 sts	87 sts	93 sts	99 sts	91 sts	101 sts	111 sts	121 sts
Work in K1 P1 rib		14 rows	14 rows	16 rows	16 rows	22 rows	22 rows	22 rows	22 rows	28 rows	28 rows	28 rows	28 rows
										increasing 16sts in the last row			
Change to 4mm needles and work in stocking stitch (standard)		64 rows	76 rows	98 rows	100 rows	116 rows	128 rows	140 rows	152 rows	156 rows	156 rows	156 rows	156 rows
Change to 4mm needles and work in stocking stitch (longer)		-	-	-	-	-	-	-	-	184 rows	184 rows	184 rows	184 rows
Change to 3.25mm needles and work in K1 P1 rib		6 rows	6 rows	6 rows	6 rows	8 rows	8 rows	8 rows	8 rows	10 rows	10 rows	10 rows	10 rows
Cast off loosely in rib													

DOUBLE-KNIT SLASH NECK contd

SLEEVES												
Using 3.25mm needles, cast on	39 sts	41 sts	43 sts	45 sts	47 sts	49 sts	51 sts	53 sts	55 sts	55 sts	55 sts	55 sts
Work in K1 P1 rib	14 rows	14 rows	16 rows	16 rows	22 rows	22 rows	22 rows	22 rows	28 rows	28 rows	28 rows	28 rows
Change to 4mm needles and work in stocking stitch increasing 1 stitch at the end of the next row, and then every 4th row to	53 sts	59 sts	65 sts	71 sts	79 sts	85 sts	91 sts	97 sts	111 sts	111 sts	111 sts	111 sts
Continue without shaping until sleeve measures cm	21	24	27	30	34	38	42	46	52	52	52	52
"	8.25	9.5	10.5	11.75	13.5	15	16.5	18	20.5	20.5	20.5	20.5
TO MAKE UP Join shoulder seams												
Measure down from shoulder seam and place markers on the side seams cm	12	13	14	16	18	19	20.5	22	25	25	25	25
"	4.75	5	5.5	6.25	7	7.5	8.25	8.75	9.75	9.75	9.75	9.75

Back stitch sleeves into position between the front and the back markers.
Sew up side and sleeve seams using back or ladder stitch.

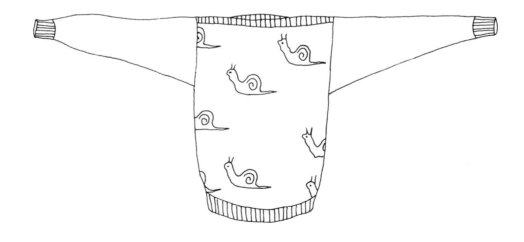

21

MOHAIR ROUND NECK

Use 4mm (8) needles for ribs and 5mm (6) needles for stocking stitch.
Knit a tension square.
The correct tension is 18 stitches and 22 rows to 10cm (4").

SIZES		SMALL	MEDIUM	LARGE
FINISHED SIZE	cm	102	112	127
	"	40	44	50
SLEEVE LENGTH	cm	52	52	52
	"	20.5	20.5	20.5
FINISHED BACK LENGTH (standard)	cm	69	69	69
	"	27	27	27
FINISHED BACK LENGTH (longer)	cm	76	76	76
	"	30	30	30
BACK				
Using 4mm needles cast on		75sts	81sts	89sts
Work in knit 1 purl 1 rib increasing 16 sts in last row *		16 rows	16 rows	16 rows
Change to 5mm needles and work in stocking stitch (standard length)		120 rows	120 rows	120 rows
Change to 5mm needles and work in stocking stitch (longer length)		140 rows	140 rows	140 rows
Cast off		27sts	30sts	34sts
Knit		37sts	37sts	37sts
Cast off remaining		27sts	30sts	34sts
Leave 37 stitches on a spare needle				
FRONT				
Knit as for back to *				
Change to 5mm needles and work in stocking stitch (standard length)		110 rows	110 rows	110 rows
Change to 5mm needles and work in stocking stitch (longer length)		130 rows	130 rows	130 rows

MOHAIR ROUND NECK contd

TO SHAPE NECK			
Knit	34sts	37sts	41sts
Knit 2 together, turn, purl 2 together. Working on these stitches decrease 1 stitch at the neck edge on the next	7 rows	7 rows	7 rows
Purl 1 row			
Cast off remaining	27sts	30sts	34sts
Slip the next 19 stitches on to a spare needle. Rejoin yarn to the next stitch and work the second side to match the first, reversing all shapings.			
NECKBAND Join right shoulder. With right side facing and using 4mm needles, pick up and knit	11 sts along left side of neck 19 sts from the centre front 12 sts along right side of neck 37 sts from the back neck(79sts) Work 5 rows in knit 1 purl 1 rib Cast off very loosely in rib. Join left shoulder.		
SLEEVES Using 4mm needles cast on	45sts	45sts	45sts
Work in knit 1, purl 1 rib increasing in alternate stitches on the last row.	16 rows	16 rows	16 rows
Change to 5mm needles and work in stocking stitch.	56 rows	56 rows	56 rows
Increase 1 stitch at each end of the next and every following alternate row to	111sts	111sts	111sts
Cast off loosely			
TO MAKE UP Measure 30cm (12") down from the shoulder seams and place markers on the side seams. Back stitch sleeves into position between front and back markers. Sew up sleeve and side seams using back or ladder stitch.			

MOHAIR SLASH NECK

Use 4mm (8) needles for ribs and 5mm (6) needles for stocking stitch.
Knit a tension square.
The correct tension is 18 stitches and 22 rows to 10cm (4").

SIZES		SMALL	MEDIUM	LARGE
FINISHED SIZE	cm	102	112	127
	"	40	44	50
SLEEVE LENGTH	cm	52	52	52
	"	20.5	20.5	20.5
FINISHED BACK LENGTH (standard)	cm	69	69	69
	"	27	27	27
FINISHED BACK LENGTH (longer)	cm	76	76	76
	"	30	30	30
BACK & FRONT (ALIKE)				
Using 4mm needles cast on		75sts	81sts	89sts
Work in knit 1 purl 1 rib increasing 16 sts in last row		16 rows	16 rows	16 rows
Change to 5mm needles and work in stocking stitch (standard length)		120 rows	120 rows	120 rows
Change to 5mm needles and work in stocking stitch (longer length)		140 rows	140 rows	140 rows
Change to 4mm needles and work in knit 1, purl 1 rib		8 rows	8 rows	8 rows
Cast off loosely in rib				
SLEEVES				
Using 4mm needles cast on		45sts	45sts	45sts
Work in knit 1, purl 1 rib, increasing in alternate stitches on the last row. (67 stitches)		16 rows	16 rows	16 rows
Change to 5mm needles and work in stocking stitch		56 rows	56 rows	56 rows
Increase one stitch at each end of the next and every following alternate row to		111sts	111sts	111sts

MOHAIR SLASH NECK contd

Cast off loosely	

TO MAKE UP

Join shoulder seams leaving approximately 24cm (9.5") at the centre. Measure 30cm (12") down from the shoulder seam and place markers on the side seams. Back stitch sleeves into position between front and back markers. Sew up sleeve and side seams, using back or ladder stitch.

ARAN ROUND NECK

Use 4mm (8) needles for ribs and 5mm (6) needles for stocking stitch.
Knit a tension square.
The correct tension is 18 stitches and 24 rows to 10cm (4").

SIZES		SMALL	MEDIUM	LARGE
FINISHED SIZE	cm	102	112	127
	"	40	44	50
SLEEVE LENGTH	cm	50	50	50
	"	19.5	19.5	19.5
FINISHED BACK LENGTH (standard)	cm	58	58	58
	"	23	23	23
FINISHED BACK LENGTH (longer)	cm	66	66	66
	"	26	26	26
BACK				
Using 4mm needles cast on		75sts	81sts	89sts
Work in knit 1 purl 1 rib		15 rows	15 rows	15 rows
Work 1 row in rib increasing		16sts	16sts	16sts
Change to 5mm needles and working in stocking stitch knit		120 rows	120 rows	120 rows
For the longer length knit		140 rows	140 rows	140 rows
Cast off		27sts	30sts	34sts
Knit		37sts	37sts	37sts
Cast off remaining		27sts	30sts	34sts
Leave 37 stitches on a spare needle				

ARAN ROUND NECK contd

FRONT			
Using 4mm needles cast on	75sts	81sts	89sts
Work in knit 1, purl 1 rib	15 rows	15 rows	15 rows
Work 1 row in rib increasing	16sts	16sts	16sts
Change to 5mm needles and working in stocking stitch knit	110 rows	110 rows	110 rows
For longer length knit	130 rows	130 rows	130 rows
TO SHAPE NECK			
Knit	34sts	37sts	41sts
Knit 2 together, turn, purl 2 together. Purl to end. Working on these stitches decrease 1 stitch at the neck edge on the next 7 rows.	27sts	30sts	34sts
Purl 1 row. Cast off			
Slip next 19sts on to a spare needle			
Rejoin yarn to next stitch and work second side to match the first reversing all the shapings.			
NECKBAND Join the right shoulder.			
With right side facing and using 4mm needles, pick up and knit along left side of neck	11sts	11sts	11sts
...from the centre front	19sts	19sts	19sts
...along the right side of neck	12sts	12sts	12sts
...and from the back neck	37sts	37sts	37sts
Total	79sts	79sts	79sts
In knit 1, purl 1 rib, work	5 rows	5 rows	5 rows
Cast off very loosely in rib.			

ARAN ROUND NECK contd.

Work without shaping for (or required length)	21 rows	21 rows	21 rows
Cast off loosely			

MAKING UP

Join the left shoulder and neckband.
Measure 30cm (12") down from the shoulder seams and place markers on the side seams. Back stitch sleeves into position between front and back markers. Sew up sleeve and side seams using back or ladder stitch.

SLEEVES			
Using 4mm needles cast on	45sts	45sts	45sts
Work in knit 1, purl 1 rib	15 rows	15 rows	15 rows
Work 1 row in rib, increasing in alternate stitches	67sts	67sts	67sts
Change to 5mm needles. In stocking stitch work	4 rows	4 rows	4 rows
Increase 1 stitch at each end of next row, and work	3 rows	3 rows	3 rows
Repeat the last four rows to	103sts	103sts	103sts

ARAN SLASH NECK

Use 4mm (8) needles for ribs and 5mm (6) needles for stocking stitch.
Knit a tension square.
The correct tension is 18 stitches and 24 rows to 10cm (4").

SIZES		SMALL	MEDIUM	LARGE
FINISHED SIZE	cm	102	112	127
	"	40	44	50
SLEEVE LENGTH	cm	50	50	50
	"	19.5	19.5	19.5
FINISHED BACK LENGTH (standard)	cm	58	58	58
	"	23	23	23

ARAN SLASH NECK contd

FINISHED BACK LENGTH cm (longer)	66	66	66
"	26	26	26
BACK & FRONT (ALIKE)			
Using 4mm needles cast on	75sts	81sts	89sts
Work in knit 1 purl 1 rib	15 rows	15 rows	15 rows
Work one row in rib increasing	16sts	16sts	16sts
Change to 5mm needles and work in stocking stitch (standard length)	120 rows	120 rows	120 rows
Change to 5mm needles and work in stocking stitch (longer length)	140 rows	140 rows	140 rows
Change to 4mm needles and work in rib for	8 rows	8 rows	8 rows
Cast off loosely in rib			
SLEEVES			
Using 4mm needles cast on	45sts	45sts	45sts
Work in knit 1, purl 1 rib,	15 rows	15 rows	15 rows
Work 1 row in rib, increasing in alternate stitches	67sts	67sts	67sts
Change to 5mm needles and work in stocking stitch	4 rows	4 rows	4 rows
Increase one stitch at each end of the next row, then work	3 rows	3 rows	3 rows
Repeat the last four rows to	103sts	103sts	103sts
Work without shaping for (or required length)	21 rows	21 rows	21 rows
Cast off loosely			

TO MAKE UP

Join shoulder seams leaving approximately 24cm (9.5") at the centre. Measure 30cm (12") down from the shoulder seam and place markers on the side seams. Back stitch sleeves into position between front and back markers. Sew up sleeve and side seams, using back or ladder stitch.

Man in the Moon (page 102) and Mr French
Mouse (page 48)

MACHINE KNIT 4-PLY ROUND NECK

Tension - 30 stitches & 40 rows to 10cm (4")
Tension dial setting - approx.6.

TO FIT		CHILDREN				ADULTS			
SIZES	cm	66	71	76	81				
	"	26	28	30	32	S	M	L	XL
FINISHED SIZE	cm	72	78	83	88	94	102	110	117
	"	28.5	31	32.5	34.5	37	40	43	46
SLEEVE LENGTH	cm	36	41	43	46	56	56	56	56
	"	14	16	17	18	22	22	22	22
FINISHED BACK LENGTH	cm	41	48	52	56	69	69	69	69
	"	16	19	20.5	22	27	27	27	27
BACK No. of stitches for the body section		109	117	125	133	141	153	165	177
No. of rows in rib		26	28	30	32	32	32	32	32
No. of rows in stocking stitch		-	-	-	-	136	136	136	136
Cast off stitches at start of next two rows		-	-	-	-	8	8	8	8
Continue without further shaping to row		-	-	-	-	240	240	240	240
SHOULDER SHAPINGS cast off		9 x 4	10 x 4	12 x 4	13 x 6	11 x 4	13 x 4	15 x 4	17 x 4
		10 x 2	12 x 2	11 x 2	-	10 x 2	12 x 2	14 x 2	16 x 2
Knit stitches on to waste yarn for the neckband		53	53	55	55	61	61	61	61
FRONT Knitted as for back to row		130	154	170	186	216	216	216	216

MACHINE KNIT 4-PLY ROUND NECK contd

Hold centre stitches	25	25	27	27	31	31	31	31
and left side stitches	42	46	49	53	47	53	59	65
Continue on right stitches	42	46	49	53	47	53	59	65
Decrease 1 stitch at neck edge on the next	10 rows	10 rows	10 rows	10 rows	10 rows	10 rows	10 rows	10 rows
Decrease at neck edge on alternate rows	4 times	4 times	4 times	4 times	5 times	5 times	5 times	5 times
Knit without further shaping to row counter	150	174	190	206	240	240	240	240
Shape shoulders by casting off on alternate rows	9 x 2	10 x 2	12 x 2	13 x 3	11 x 2	13 x 2	15 x 2	17 x 2
	10 x 1	12 x 1	11 x 1	-	10 x 1	12 x 1	14 x 1	16 x 1
Knit centre sts on to waste	25	25	27	27	31	31	31	31

Knit second side to match the first, reversing all shapings.
Join right shoulder.

NECKBAND Cast on in rib	121 sts	121 sts	121 sts	121 sts	121 sts	121 sts	121 sts	121 sts
Number of rows for neckband	16	16	16	16	18	18	18	18

With wrong side facing you, pick the stitches up on the neck and place evenly on to the needles. Knit 1 row at tension 8. & 1 row at tension 10. Cast off using a latch tool

SLEEVES No. of stitches	59	61	63	65	71	71	71	71
No. of rows in rib	26	28	30	32	32	32	32	32
Increase 1 stitch at each end of every 4th row to	99	107	115	127	143	143	143	143

MACHINE KNIT 4-PLY ROUND NECK contd

Knit without further shaping to row counter	126	146	156	166	200	200	200	200
Cast off loosely								
TO MAKE UP Join shoulder seams								

Measure down from shoulder seam and place markers on the side seams	cm	17	18	19	21	-	-	-	-
	"	6.75	7	7.5	8.25	-	-	-	-

Back stitch sleeves into position between the front and the back markers or shapings. Sew up side and sleeve seams using back or ladder stitch.
SLIP STITCH NECKBAND ON TO THE WRONG SIDE.

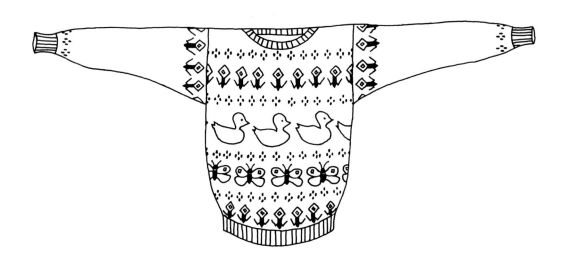

MACHINE KNIT 4-PLY SLASH NECK

Tension - 30 stitches & 40 rows to 10cm (4")
Tension dial setting - approx 6.

TO FIT		TODDLERS				CHILDREN				ADULTS			
SIZES cm		46	51	56	61	66	71	76	81				
"		18	20	22	24	26	28	30	32	S	M	L	XL
FINISHED SIZE cm		53	58	63	68	72	78	83	88	94	102	110	117
"		21	23	25	27	28.5	31	32.5	34.5	37	40	43	46
SLEEVE LENGTH cm		20	22.5	26	31	36	41	43	46	56	56	56	56
"		8	9	10.5	12.5	14	16	17	18	22	22	22	22
FINISHED BACK LENGTH cm		22.5	30	32	36	41	48	52	56	69	69	69	69
"		10	12	13	14.5	16	19	20.5	22	27	27	27	27
BACK & FRONT No. of stitches for body sections		79	87	95	103	109	117	125	133	141	153	165	177
No. of rows in rib		18	20	22	24	26	28	30	32	32	32	32	32
No. of rows in stocking stitch		80	100	110	128	144	168	184	200	136	136	136	136
Cast off stitches at start of next two rows		-	-	-	-	-	-	-	-	8	8	8	8
Continue without further shaping to row counter		-	-	-	-	-	-	-	-	240	240	240	240
No. of rows in rib for the shoulder		16	16	16	16	16	16	16	16	18	18	18	18

Pick up stitches from the last row of stocking stitch and put them on to the corresponding needles. Knit one row at tension 10. Cast off using a latch tool.

SLEEVES													
No. of stitches for the sleeves		51	53	55	57	59	61	63	65	71	71	71	71
No. of rows in rib.		18	20	22	24	26	28	30	32	32	32	32	32

MACHINE KNIT 4-PLY SLASH NECK contd

Increase 1 stitch at each end of every 4th row to	69	77	85	93	99	107	115	127	143	143	143	143
Knit without further shaping to row counter	72	82	90	106	126	146	156	166	200	200	200	200

Cast off loosely

TO MAKE UP					Join shoulder seams							
Measure down from shoulder seam and place markers on the side seams cm	12	13	14	16	17	18	18	21	-	-	-	-
"	4.75	5	5.5	6.25	6.75	7	7.5	8.25	-	-	-	-

Back stitch sleeves into position between the front and the back markers or shapings. Sew up side and sleeve seams using back or ladder stitch.

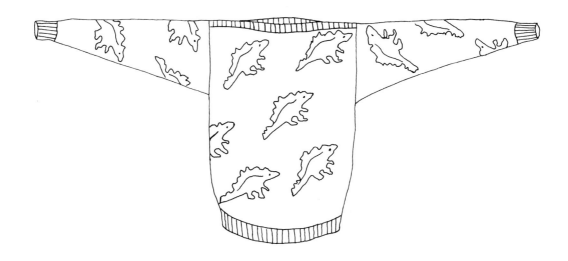

ROUND NECK JUMPER FOR CHUNKY MACHINES

Mohair or Aran yarns may be used to knit this pattern, but a tension of 18 stitches and 22 rows must be achieved before the garment is made (approx. tension 4.)

TO FIT		ONE SIZE
FINISHED SIZE	cm	100
	"	40
SLEEVE LENGTH	cm	52
	"	20.5
FINISHED BACK LENGTH (standard)	cm	69
	"	27
FINISHED BACK LENGTH (longer)	cm	76
	"	30
BACK		
With waste yarn, cast on and knit a few rows ending at the right		91sts
Set row counter to 000 and knit in the main yarn		120 rows
For the longer length, knit		140 rows
Cast off		27sts
Knit the next on to waste yarn for the back neck		37sts
Cast off remaining		27sts
FRONT		
With waste yarn cast on		91sts
Set row counter to 000 and knit in the main yarn		110 rows
For the longer length knit		130 rows
Push into holding position the left		55sts
Knit one row over the remaining		36sts

ROUND NECK JUMPER FOR CHUNKY MACHINES contd

Decrease one stitch at the neck edge on the next	9 rows
Cast off the remaining	27sts
Knit the next on to waste yarn	19sts

Knit the second side to match the first reversing all shapings

SLEEVES With waste yarn, cast on and knit a few rows ending at the right	65sts
Set row counter to 000 and knit in the main yarn (length may be adjusted here)	56 rows
Increase one stitch at the beginning of every row to	109sts

Knit 1 row on the maximum tension and cast off using the latch tool

ALTERNATIVE SLEEVE PATTERN With waste yarn, cast on and knit a few rows ending at the right	65sts
Set row counter to 000 and knit in the main yarn	4 rows
Increase one stitch at each end and knit	4 rows
Repeat the last four rows to	109sts
Continue without shaping to row counter	100

Knit 1 row on the maximum tension and cast off using the latch tool

CUFFS Pick up the first row of the main yarn on to a 4mm knitting needle and knit in K1 P1 rib decreasing evenly along the row.	20sts
No. of stitches remaining on needle	44sts

ROUND NECK JUMPER FOR CHUNKY MACHINES contd

Knit a further 16 rows in K1 P1 rib. Cast off loosely in rib.

RIBS FOR MAIN BODY (all sizes knitted the same)

Pick up the first row of the main yarn onto a 4mm knitting needle
and knit 16 rows in K1 P1 rib. Cast off loosely in rib.

NECKBAND

Join right shoulder. With right side facing and using 4mm knitting
needles, pick up and knit 11 stitches along left side of neck,
19 stitches from centre front; 12 stitches along right side of neck,
and 37 stitches from back neck (79 stitches). Work 5 rows in K1 P1
rib. Cast off very loosely in rib. Join left shoulder and neckband.

TO MAKE UP

Measure 30cm (12") down from the shoulder seam and place markers
on the side seams. Back stitch sleeves into position between front
and back markers. Sew up sleeve and side seams, using back or
ladder stitch.

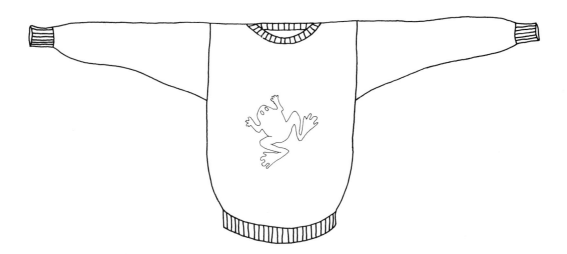

SLASH NECK JUMPER FOR CHUNKY MACHINES

Mohair or Aran yarns may be used to knit this pattern, but a tension of 18 stitches and 22 rows must be achieved before the garment is made (approx. tension 4.)

TO FIT		ONE SIZE
FINISHED SIZE	cm	100
	"	40
SLEEVE LENGTH	cm	52
	"	20.5
FINISHED BACK LENGTH (standard)	cm	69
	"	27
FINISHED BACK LENGTH (longer)	cm	76
	"	30
BACK AND FRONT With waste yarn, cast on and knit a few rows ending at the right		91sts
Set row counter to 000 & knit in the main yarn		(standard) 120 rows
		(longer) 140 rows
Remove the main yarn from the machine and transfer the stitches to a 4mm knitting needle. Knit in K1 P1 rib		8 rows
Cast off loosely in rib		
SLEEVES With waste yarn, cast on and knit a few rows ending at the right		65sts
Set row counter to 000 and knit in the main yarn (length may be adjusted here)		56 rows
Increase one stitch at the beginning of every row to		109sts
Knit 1 row on the maximum tension and cast off using the latch tool		

SLASH NECK JUMPER FOR CHUNKY MACHINES contd

ALTERNATIVE SLEEVE PATTERN With waste yarn, cast on and knit a few rows ending at the right	65sts
Set row counter to 000 and knit in the main yarn	4 rows
Increase one stitch at each end and knit	4 rows
Repeat the last four rows to	109sts
Continue without shaping to row counter	100

Knit 1 row on the maximum tension and cast off using the latch tool

CUFFS Pick up the first row of the main yarn on to a 4mm knitting needle and knit in K1 P1 rib decreasing evenly along the row.	20sts
No. of stitches remaining on needle	44sts

Knit a further 16 rows in K1 P1 rib. Cast off loosely in rib.

RIBS FOR MAIN BODY (all sizes knitted the same)

Pick up the first row of the main yarn onto a 4mm knitting needle
and knit 16 rows in K1 P1 rib. Cast off loosely in rib.

TO MAKE UP

Join shoulder seams leaving approximately 24cm (9.5") at the centre.
Measure 30cm (12") down from the shoulder seam and place markers
on the side seams. Back stitch sleeves into position between front
and back markers. Sew up sleeve and side seams, using back or
ladder stitch.

THE MOTIFS

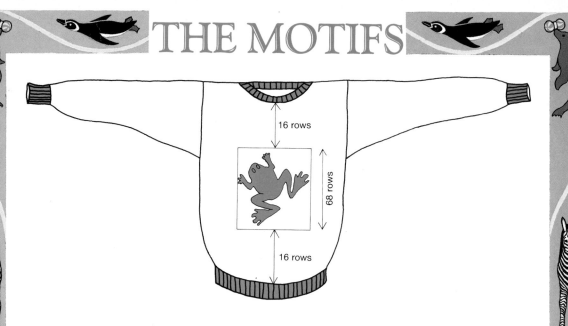

HOW TO POSITION THE MOTIFS

Where you actually position the motif is entirely up to you. Large single motifs are generally placed in the centre of the garment; scattered motifs can literally be anywhere. However the same basic rules apply to both.

CENTRAL MOTIFS

In order to position the motif centrally, you must calculate your starting row and first stitch of the motif.

To find the Starting Row Deduct the number of rows in your motif from the number of rows required in the garment, then halve this figure eg

Garment length .... 100 rows
Motif: Jumping Frog .... 68 rows
Deduct 68 from 100 .... 32 rows
Half of 32 .... 16 rows
In this case, you need to knit 16 rows before you start the motif.

To find the Starting Stitch Deduct the number of stitches on the needles, then halve the remaining figure eg

Garment width .... 75 stitches
Motif: Jumping Frog .... 55 stitches
Deduct 55 from 75 .... 20 stitches
Half of 20 .... 10 stitches
In this case, 10 stitches are knitted before using the motif graph.

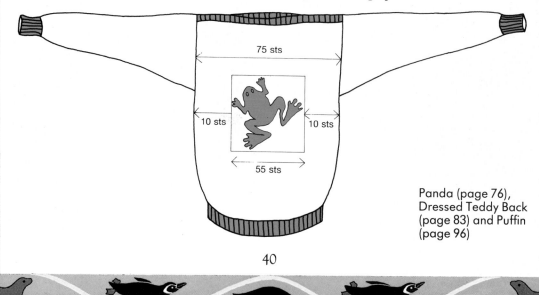

Panda (page 76),
Dressed Teddy Back
(page 83) and Puffin
(page 96)

MAIN MOTIFS

Name	Stitches	Rows	Name	Stitches	Rows
Back of Elephant	44	95	Sitting Frog	52	72
Teddy Bear	55	89	Panda	49	105
Maxwell Mouse	60	105	Jumping Frog	59	71
Mr French Mouse	56	98	Whale	60	103
Frontal Pig	30	72	Rabbit	59	75
Teddy Bear and Duck	55	94	Abigail's Elephant	44	95
Perching Owl	36	101	Dressed Teddy Front	55	94
Squatting Lion	53	90	Dressed Teddy Back	55	94
Frontal Owl	41	86	Swimming Penguins	72	82
Sitting Cat	49	99	Seal with Ball on Nose	49	97
Vole	43	89	Flamingo	45	107
Penguin	53	93	Bo Peep	46	70
Sitting Dog	55	87	Kangaroo	57	92
Monkey on Branch	73	104	Koala Bear	56	86
Teddy in Basket	43	106	Humpty Dumpty	60	103
Badger	55	37	Reindeer	54	94
Herbert Hedgehog	50	30	Dolls' House	60	105
Leaping Frog	55	68	Dinosaur	60	89
Squatting Frog	48	55	Puffin	57	92
Squirrel	50	101	Clown	37	100
Cow over the Moon	60	72	Elephant	57	100
Pig on the Wall	75	87	Pheasant	63	108
Duck	60	70	Zebra	61	75
Standing Dressed Teddy	53	100	Man in the Moon	51	94
Sheep	47	37	Mortar Board Owl	48	93
Swan	55	48	Giraffe	55	103
Scarecrow	74	100	Seal with Ball on Tail	57	88
Side Pig	57	38	Lamb	48	63
Snoozing Pig	56	30	Snowman	37	100
Polar Bear	50	87	Teddy in Stocking	33	98

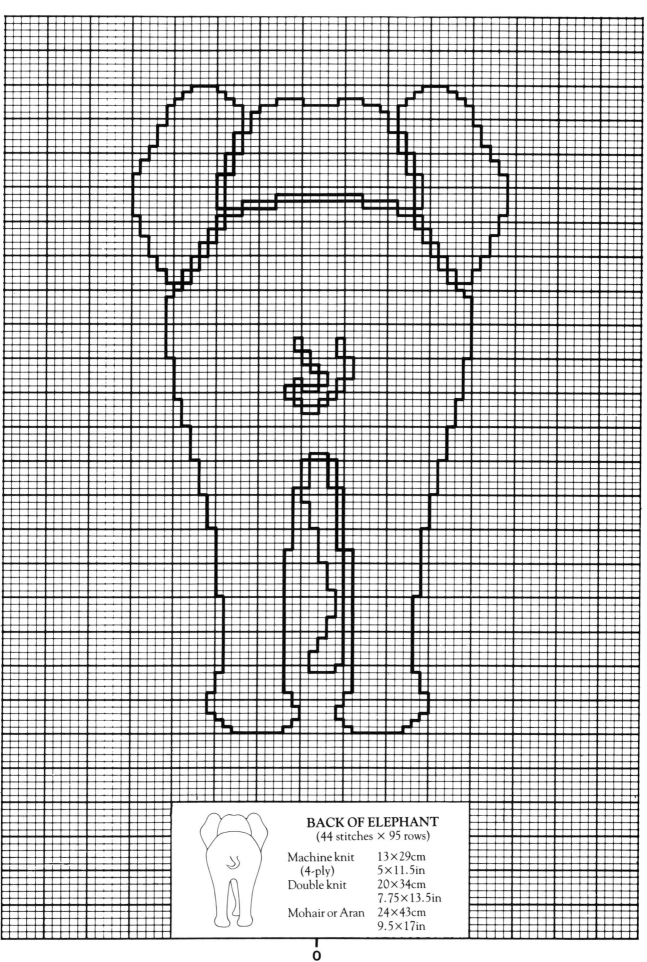

BACK OF ELEPHANT
(44 stitches × 95 rows)

Machine knit (4-ply)	13×29cm	5×11.5in
Double knit	20×34cm	7.75×13.5in
Mohair or Aran	24×43cm	9.5×17in

0

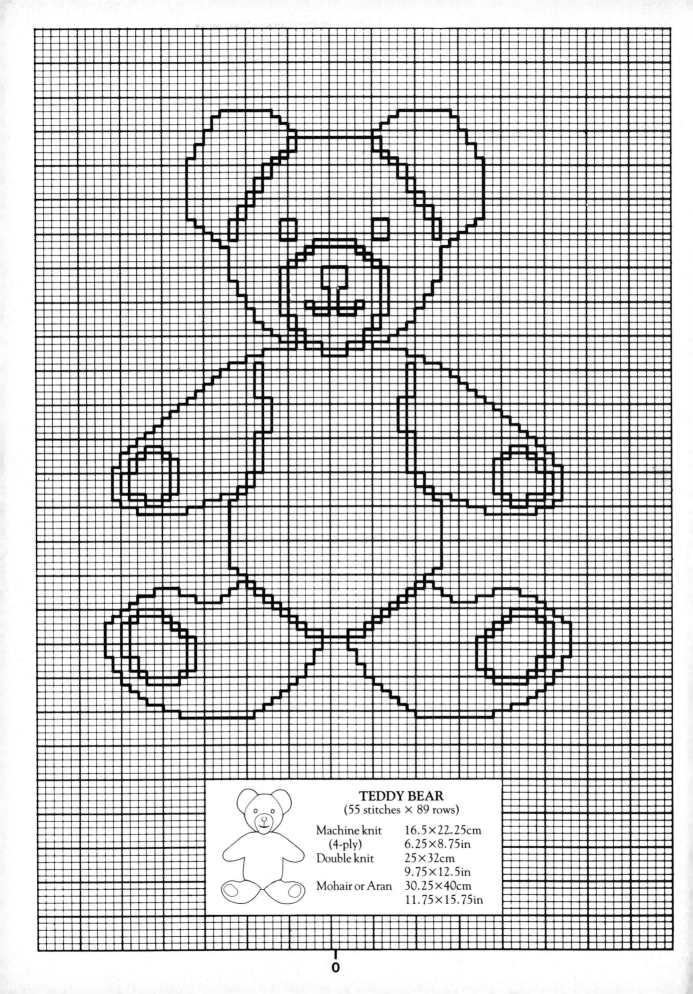

TEDDY BEAR
(55 stitches × 89 rows)

Machine knit	16.5×22.25cm	
(4-ply)	6.25×8.75in	
Double knit	25×32cm	
	9.75×12.5in	
Mohair or Aran	30.25×40cm	
	11.75×15.75in	

0

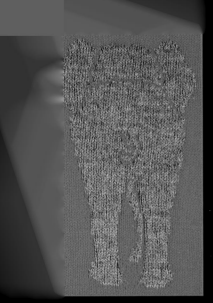

Back of Elephant (page 43)

Perching Owl (page 51)

Frontal Pig (page 46)

Flamingo (page 87)

Sitting Cat (page 55)

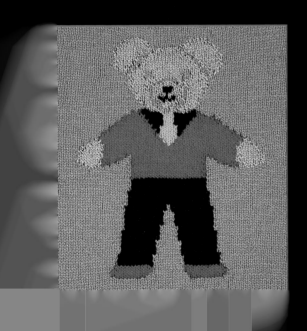

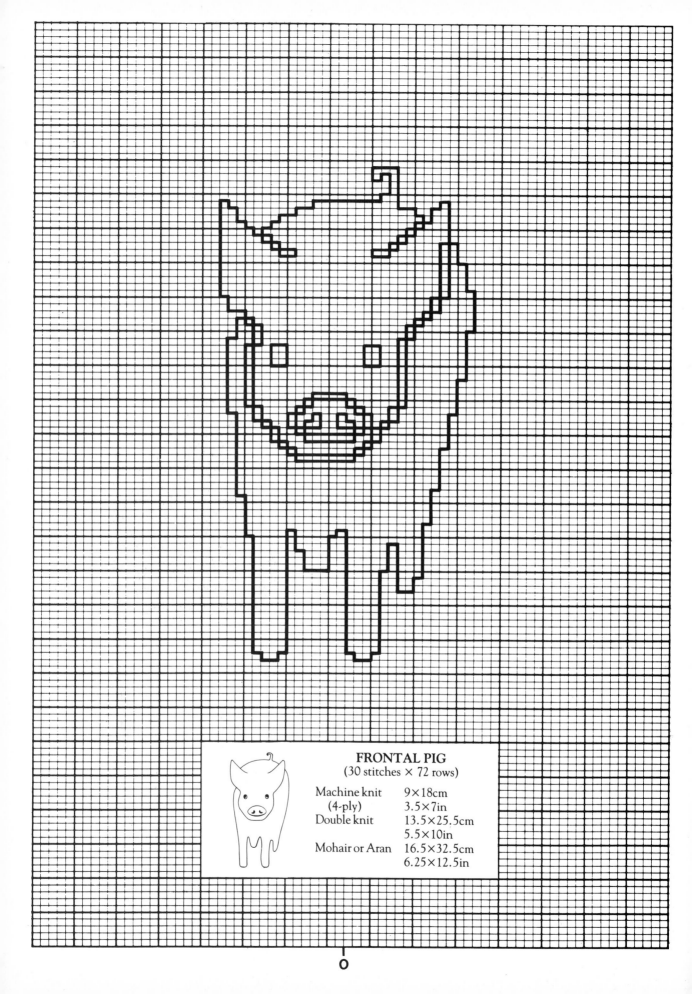

FRONTAL PIG
(30 stitches × 72 rows)

Machine knit	9×18cm	
(4-ply)	3.5×7in	
Double knit	13.5×25.5cm	
	5.5×10in	
Mohair or Aran	16.5×32.5cm	
	6.25×12.5in	

O

MAXWELL MOUSE
(60 stitches × 105 rows)

Machine knit	18×26.25cm
(4-ply)	7×10.25in
Double knit	27×38cm
	10.75×15in
Mohair or	33×47.25cm
Aran	13×18.5in

O

MR FRENCH MOUSE
(56 stitches × 98 rows)

Machine knit (4-ply)	17×24.5cm	6.75×9.5in
Double knit	25×35cm	9.75×13.75in
Mohair or Aran	31×44cm	12.25×17.25in

Jumping Frog (page 78)

Duck (page 68)

Sheep (page 71)

Mortar Board Owl (page 103)

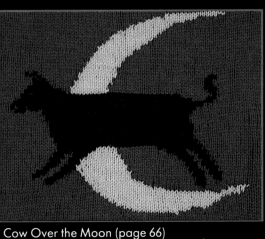

Cow Over the Moon (page 66)

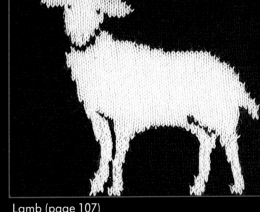

Lamb (page 107)

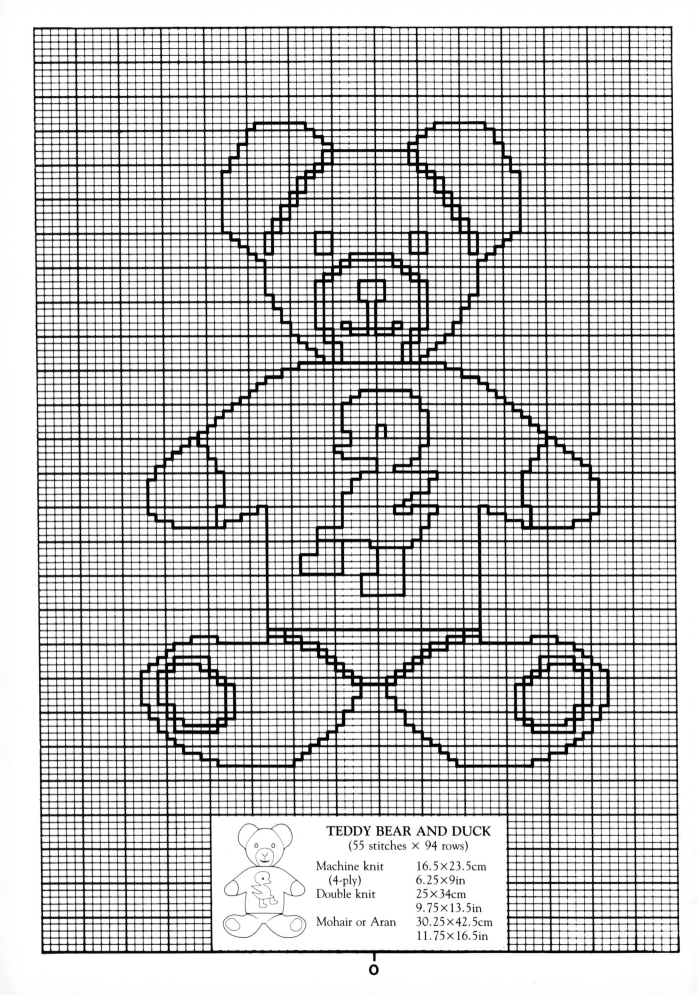

TEDDY BEAR AND DUCK
(55 stitches × 94 rows)

Machine knit	16.5×23.5cm	
(4-ply)	6.25×9in	
Double knit	25×34cm	
	9.75×13.5in	
Mohair or Aran	30.25×42.5cm	
	11.75×16.5in	

o

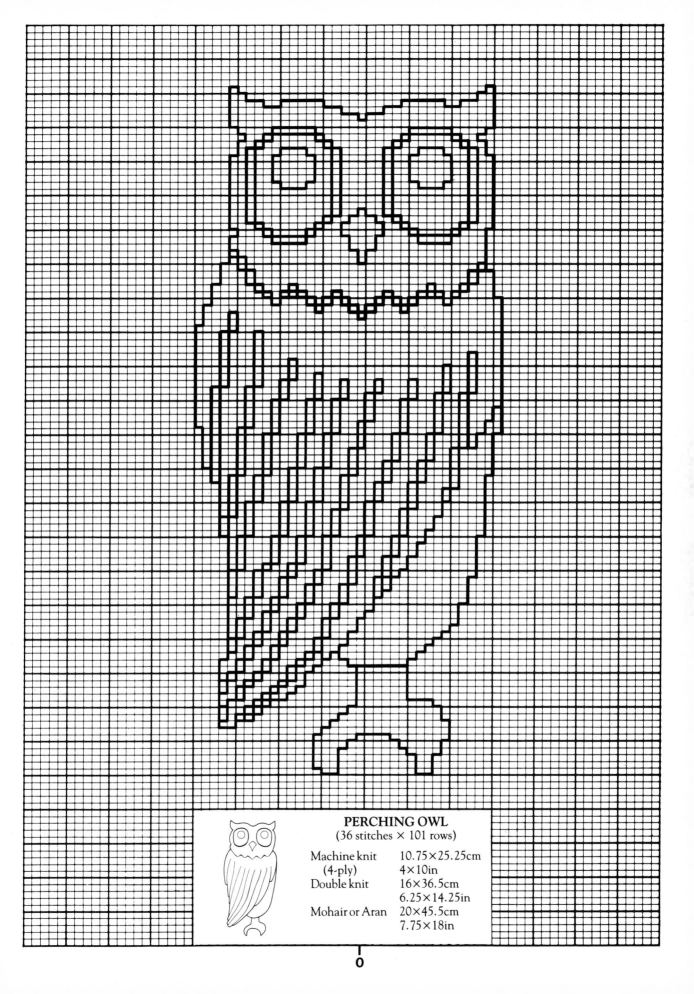

PERCHING OWL
(36 stitches × 101 rows)

Machine knit	10.75×25.25cm
(4-ply)	4×10in
Double knit	16×36.5cm
	6.25×14.25in
Mohair or Aran	20×45.5cm
	7.75×18in

SQUATTING LION
(53 stitches × 90 rows)

Machine knit	16×22.5cm	
(4-ply)	6.25×8.75in	
Double knit	24×32.5cm	
	9.5×12.5in	
Mohair or Aran	29×40.5cm	
	11.5×16in	

Teddy Bear and Duck (page 50)

Squatting Lion (page 52)

Maxwell Mouse (page 47)

Frontal Owl (page 54)

FRONTAL OWL
(41 stitches × 86 rows)

Machine knit (4-ply)	12×21.5cm 4.75×8.25in	
Double knit	18.5×31cm 7×12.25in	
Mohair or Aran	22.5×39cm 8.75×15.25in	

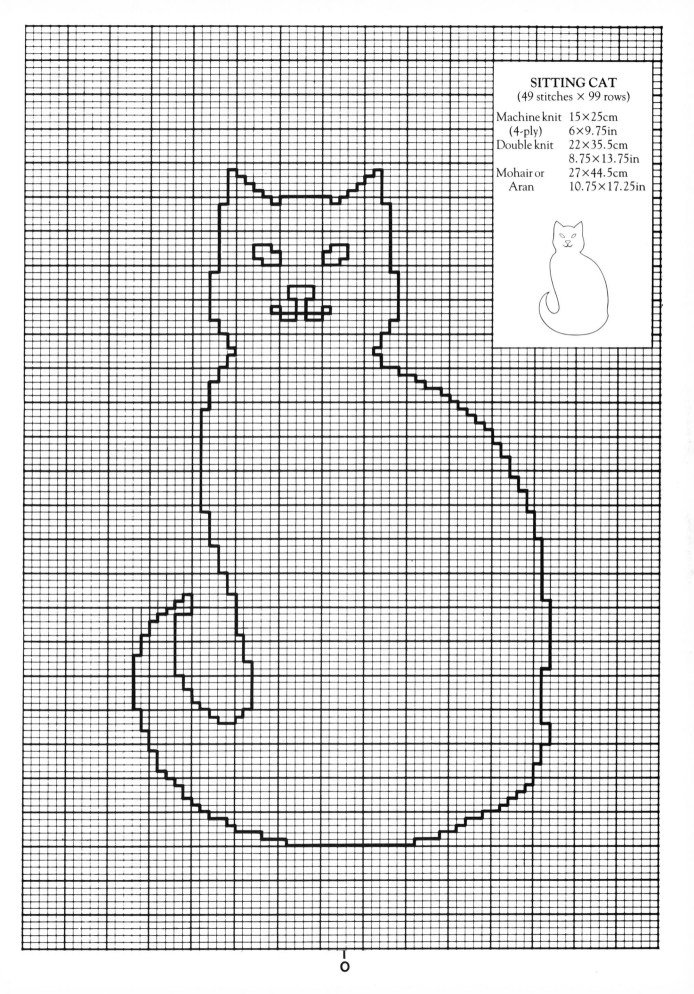

SITTING CAT
(49 stitches × 99 rows)

Machine knit	15×25cm	
(4-ply)	6×9.75in	
Double knit	22×35.5cm	
	8.75×13.75in	
Mohair or	27×44.5cm	
Aran	10.75×17.25in	

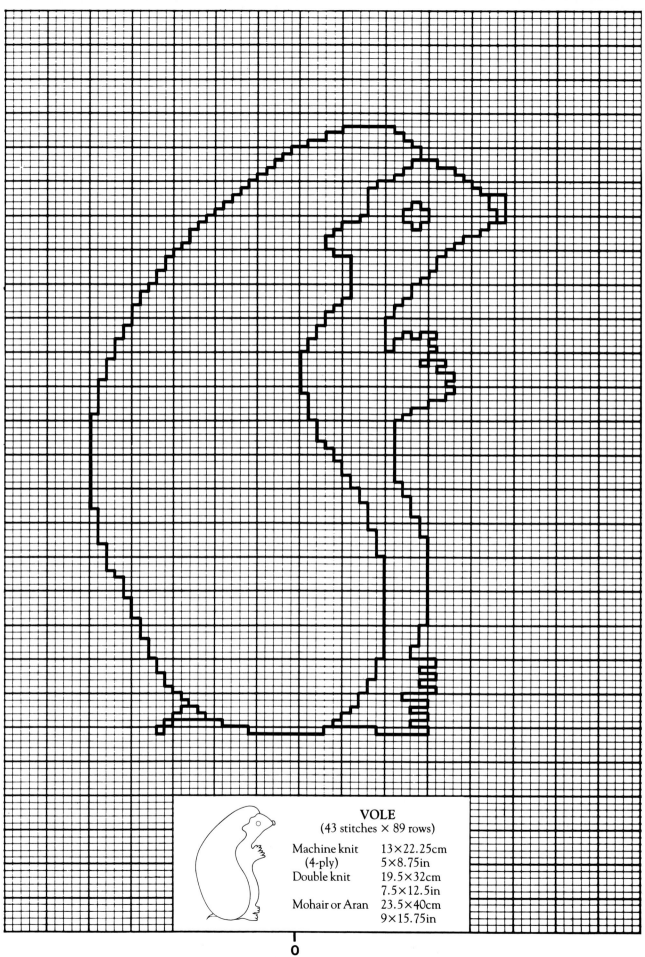

VOLE
(43 stitches × 89 rows)

Machine knit	13×22.25cm	
(4-ply)	5×8.75in	
Double knit	19.5×32cm	
	7.5×12.5in	
Mohair or Aran	23.5×40cm	
	9×15.75in	

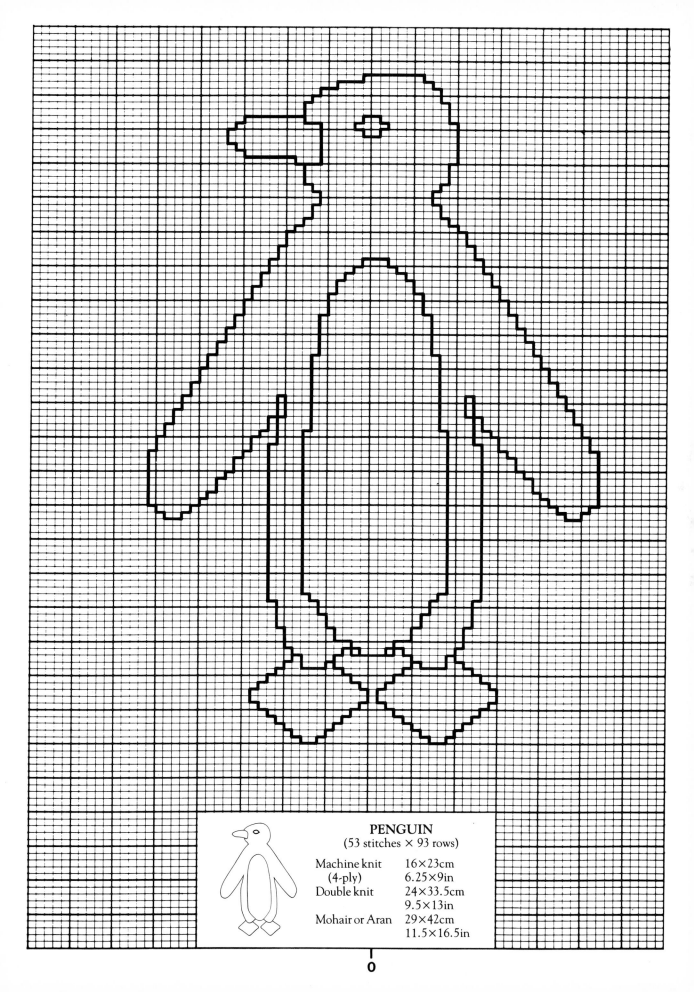

PENGUIN
(53 stitches × 93 rows)

Machine knit	16×23cm	
(4-ply)	6.25×9in	
Double knit	24×33.5cm	
	9.5×13in	
Mohair or Aran	29×42cm	
	11.5×16.5in	

0

SITTING DOG
(55 stitches × 87 rows)

Machine knit	16.5×22cm	
(4-ply)	6.5×8.75in	
Double knit	25×31cm	
	9.75×12.25in	
Mohair or Aran	30.25×39cm	
	11.75×15.25in	

0

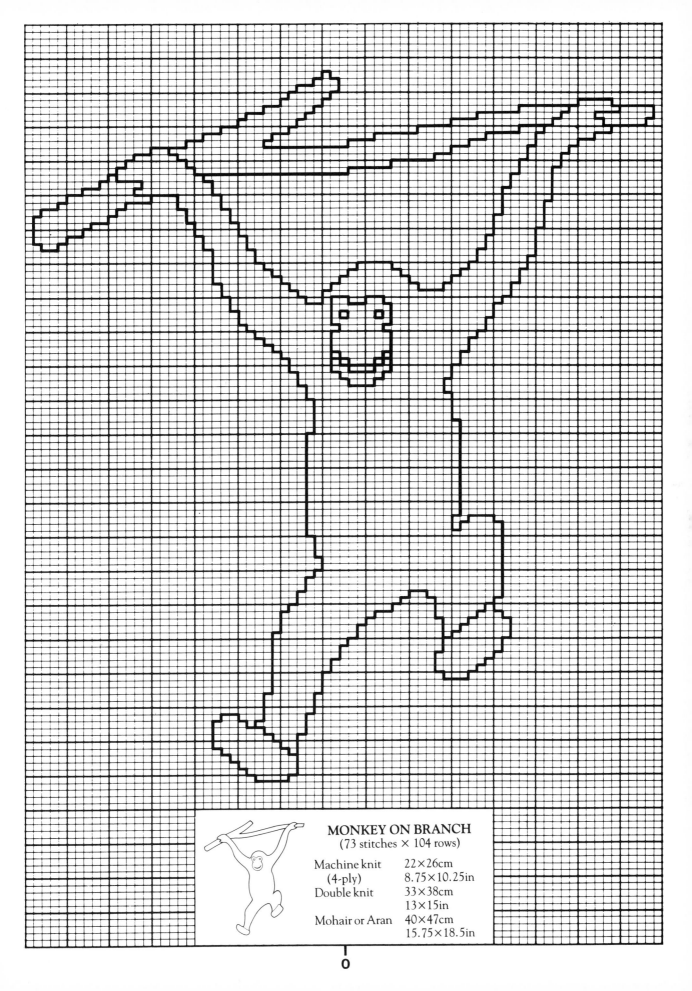

MONKEY ON BRANCH
(73 stitches × 104 rows)

Machine knit	22×26cm	
(4-ply)	8.75×10.25in	
Double knit	33×38cm	
	13×15in	
Mohair or Aran	40×47cm	
	15.75×18.5in	

0

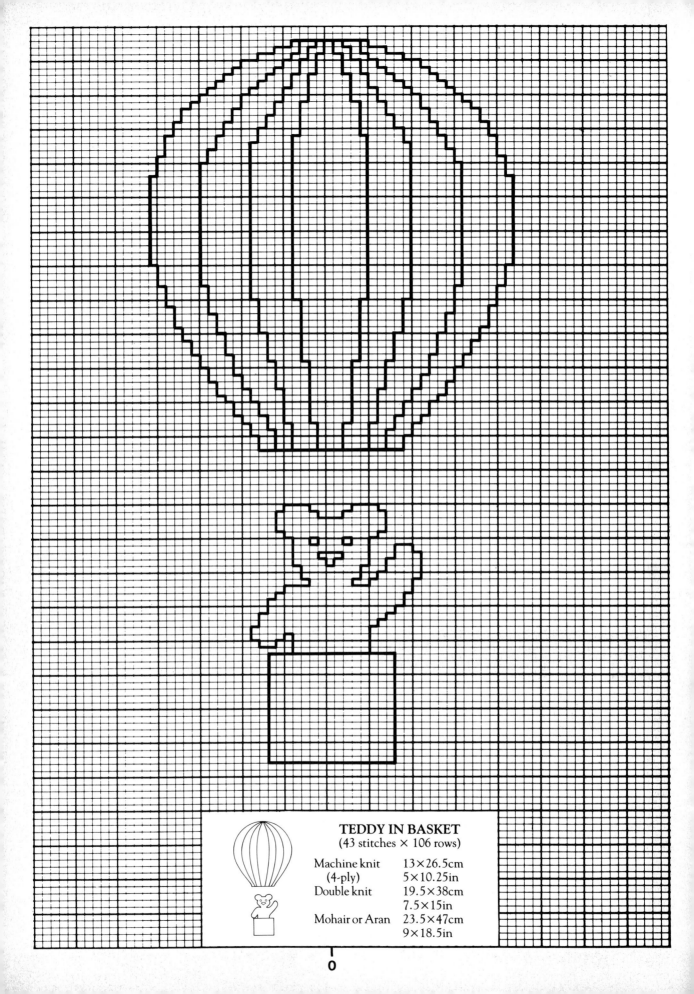

TEDDY IN BASKET
(43 stitches × 106 rows)

Machine knit	13×26.5cm	
(4-ply)	5×10.25in	
Double knit	19.5×38cm	
	7.5×15in	
Mohair or Aran	23.5×47cm	
	9×18.5in	

0

Scarecrow (page 72)

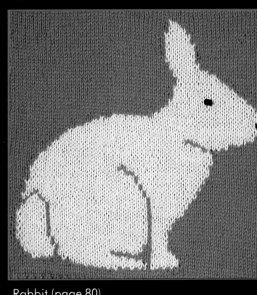

Monkey on Branch (page 59)

Mr French Mouse (page 48)

Swan (page 71)

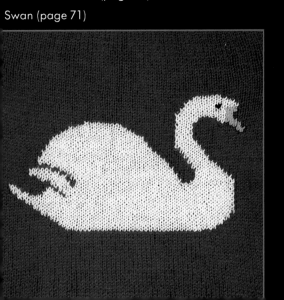

Rabbit (page 80)

Leaping Frog (page 63)

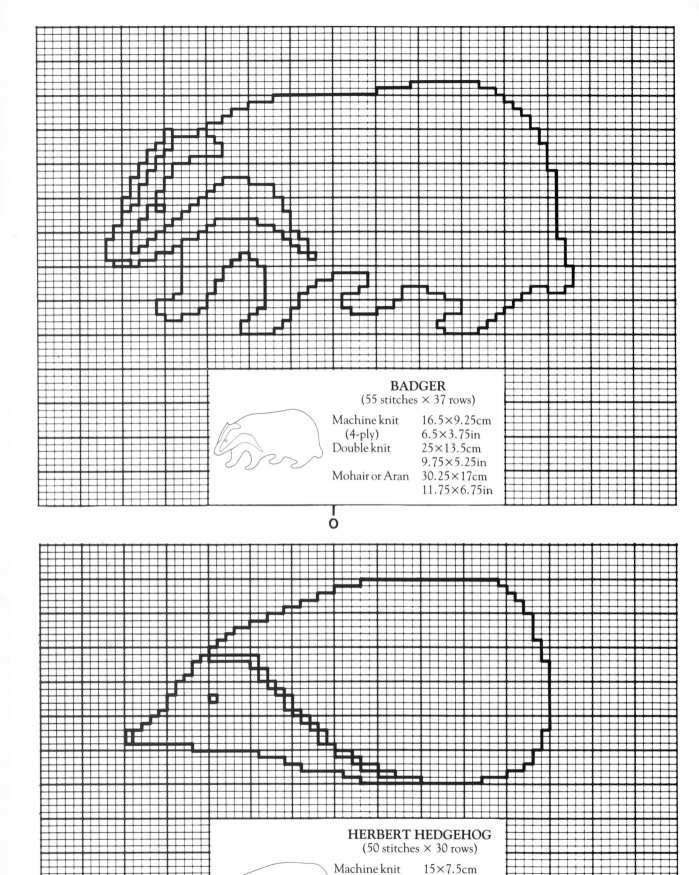

BADGER
(55 stitches × 37 rows)

Machine knit	16.5×9.25cm
(4-ply)	6.5×3.75in
Double knit	25×13.5cm
	9.75×5.25in
Mohair or Aran	30.25×17cm
	11.75×6.75in

HERBERT HEDGEHOG
(50 stitches × 30 rows)

Machine knit	15×7.5cm
(4-ply)	6×3in
Double knit	22.5×11cm
	8.75×4.25in
Mohair or Aran	27.5×13.5cm
	10.75×5.25in

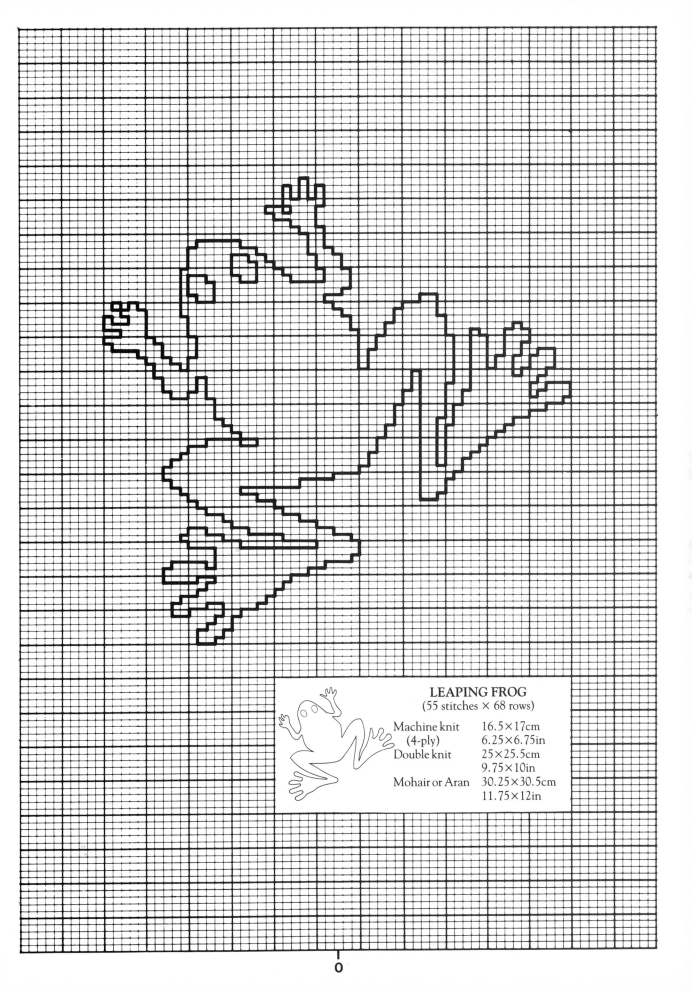

LEAPING FROG
(55 stitches × 68 rows)

Machine knit	16.5×17cm	
(4-ply)	6.25×6.75in	
Double knit	25×25.5cm	
	9.75×10in	
Mohair or Aran	30.25×30.5cm	
	11.75×12in	

0

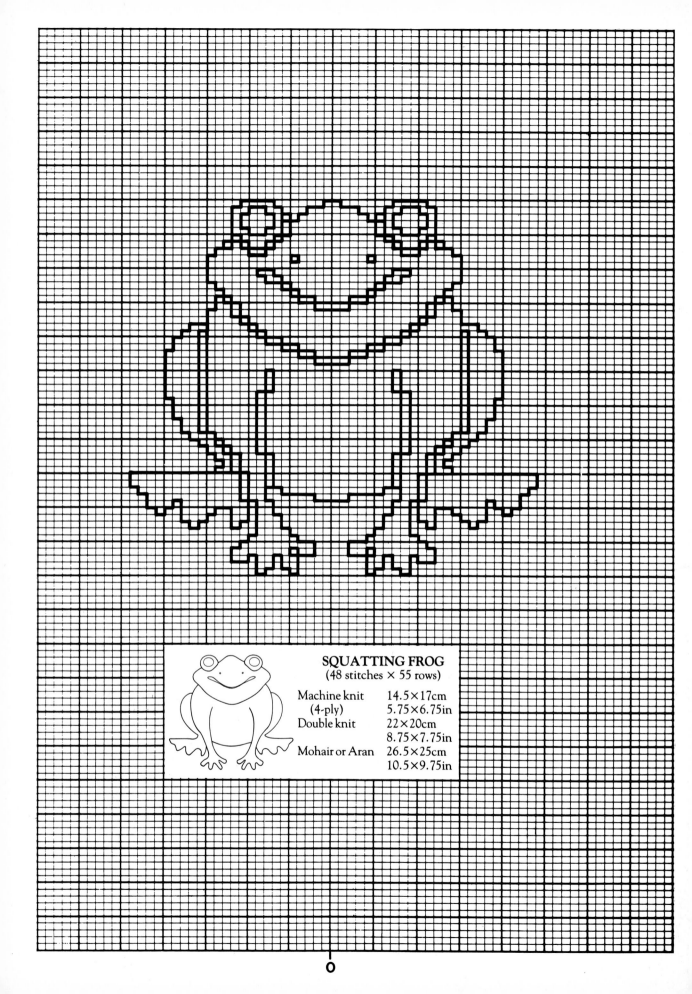

SQUATTING FROG
(48 stitches × 55 rows)

Machine knit	14.5×17cm	
(4-ply)	5.75×6.75in	
Double knit	22×20cm	
	8.75×7.75in	
Mohair or Aran	26.5×25cm	
	10.5×9.75in	

o

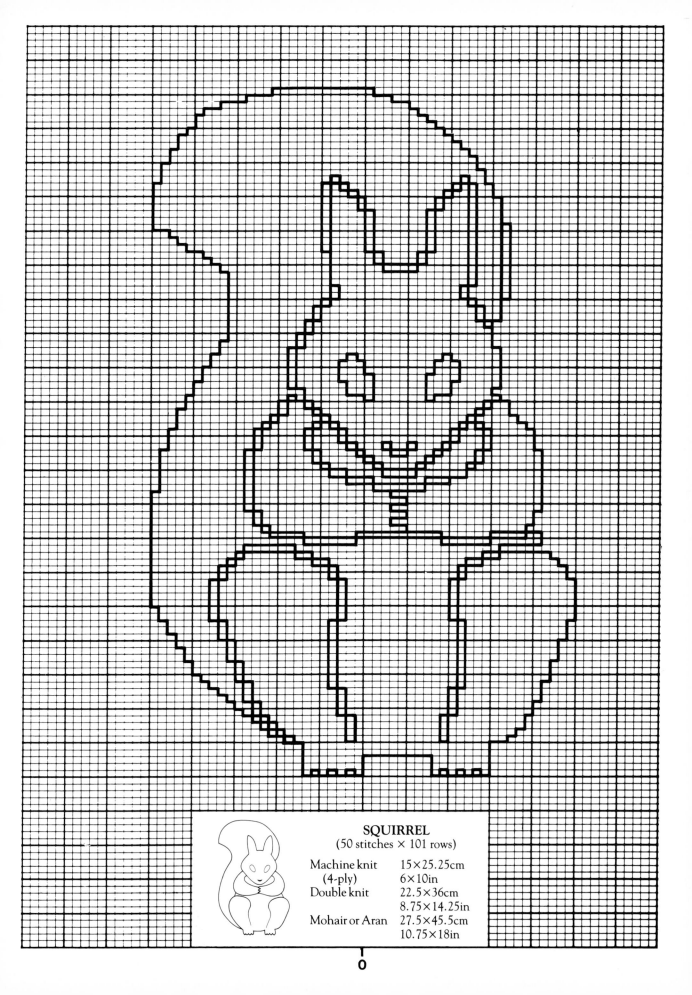

SQUIRREL
(50 stitches × 101 rows)

Machine knit	15×25.25cm	
(4-ply)	6×10in	
Double knit	22.5×36cm	
	8.75×14.25in	
Mohair or Aran	27.5×45.5cm	
	10.75×18in	

0

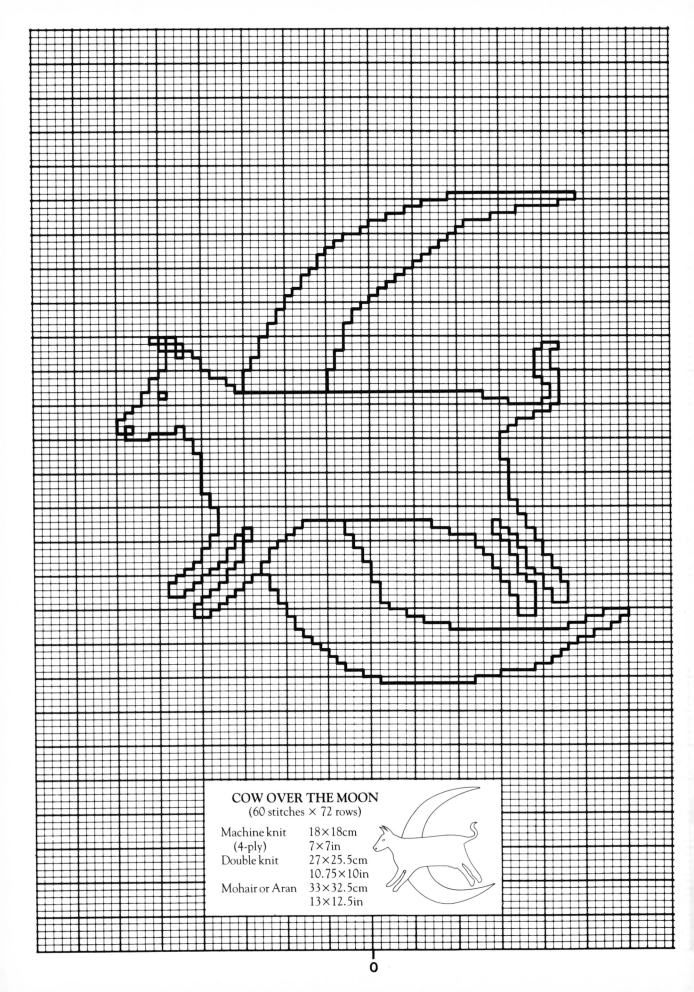

COW OVER THE MOON
(60 stitches × 72 rows)

Machine knit	18×18cm	
(4-ply)	7×7in	
Double knit	27×25.5cm	
	10.75×10in	
Mohair or Aran	33×32.5cm	
	13×12.5in	

0

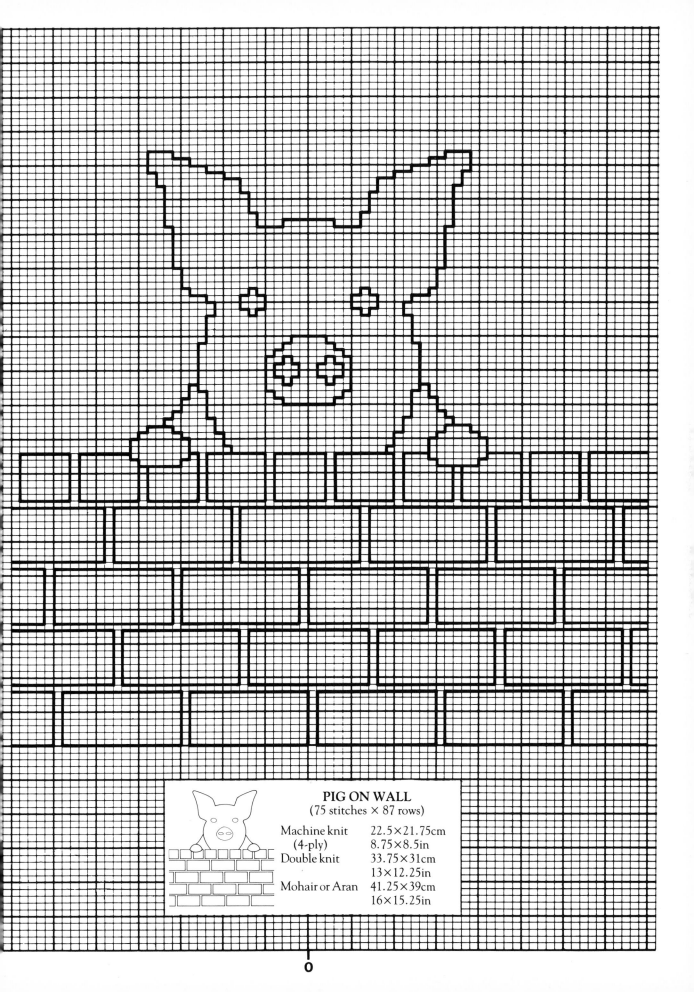

PIG ON WALL
(75 stitches × 87 rows)

Machine knit (4-ply)	22.5×21.75cm	8.75×8.5in
Double knit	33.75×31cm	13×12.25in
Mohair or Aran	41.25×39cm	16×15.25in

0

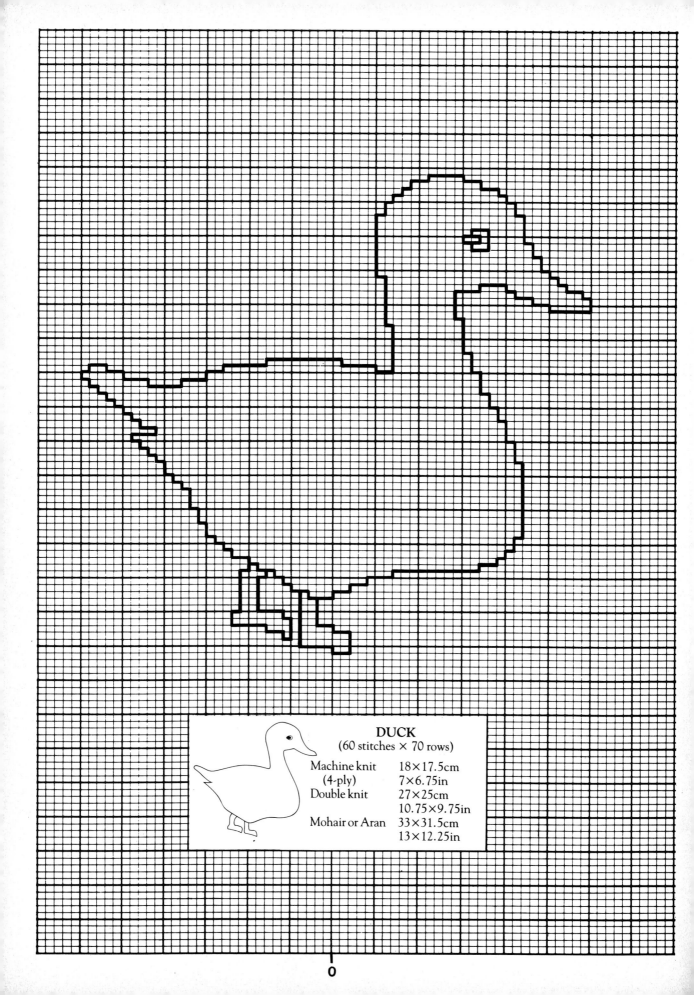

DUCK
(60 stitches × 70 rows)

Machine knit	18×17.5cm
(4-ply)	7×6.75in
Double knit	27×25cm
	10.75×9.75in
Mohair or Aran	33×31.5cm
	13×12.25in

0

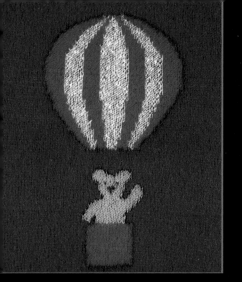

Teddy in Basket (page 60)

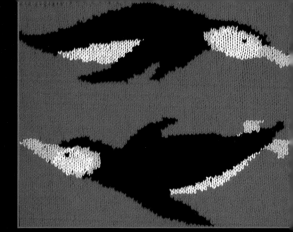

Swimming Penguins (page 84)

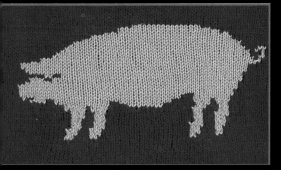

Side Pig (page 73)

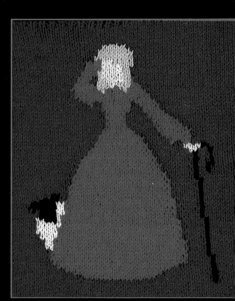

Bo Peep (page 88)

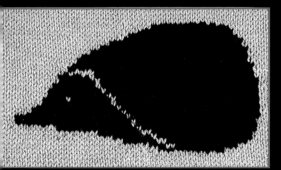

Herbert Hedgehog (page 62)

Snoozing Pig (page 73)

Dolls' House (page 94)

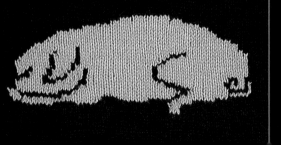

STANDING DRESSED TEDDY
(53 stitches × 100 rows)

Machine knit	16×25cm
(4-ply)	6.25×9.75in
Double knit	24×36cm
	9.25×14.25in
Mohair or Aran	29×45cm
	11.5×17.75in

0

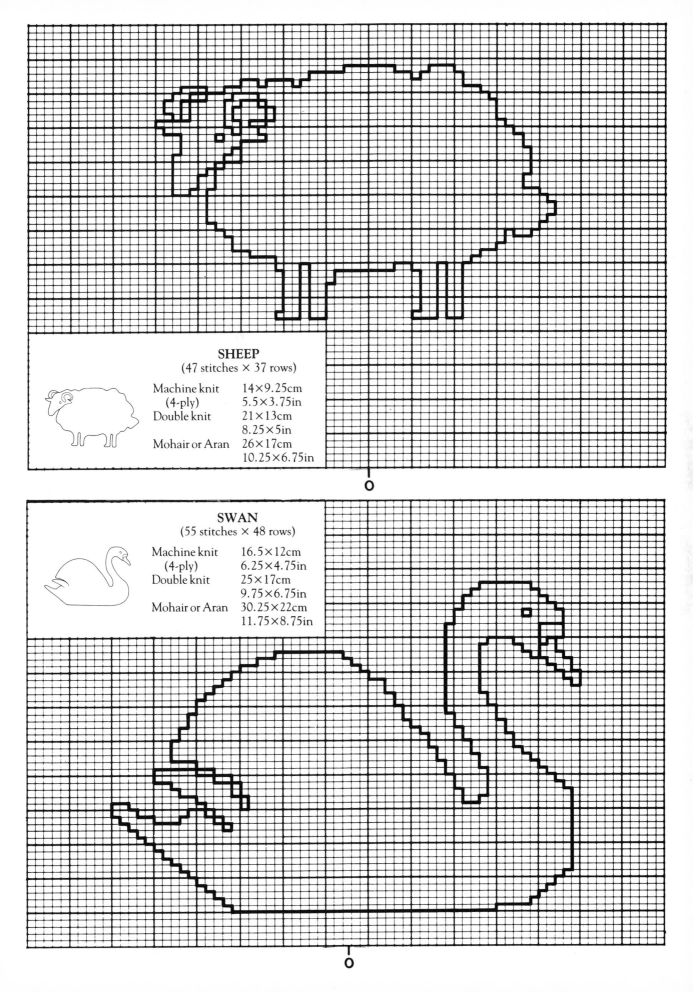

SHEEP
(47 stitches × 37 rows)

Machine knit (4-ply)	14×9.25cm 5.5×3.75in	
Double knit	21×13cm 8.25×5in	
Mohair or Aran	26×17cm 10.25×6.75in	

O

SWAN
(55 stitches × 48 rows)

Machine knit (4-ply)	16.5×12cm 6.25×4.75in	
Double knit	25×17cm 9.75×6.75in	
Mohair or Aran	30.25×22cm 11.75×8.75in	

O

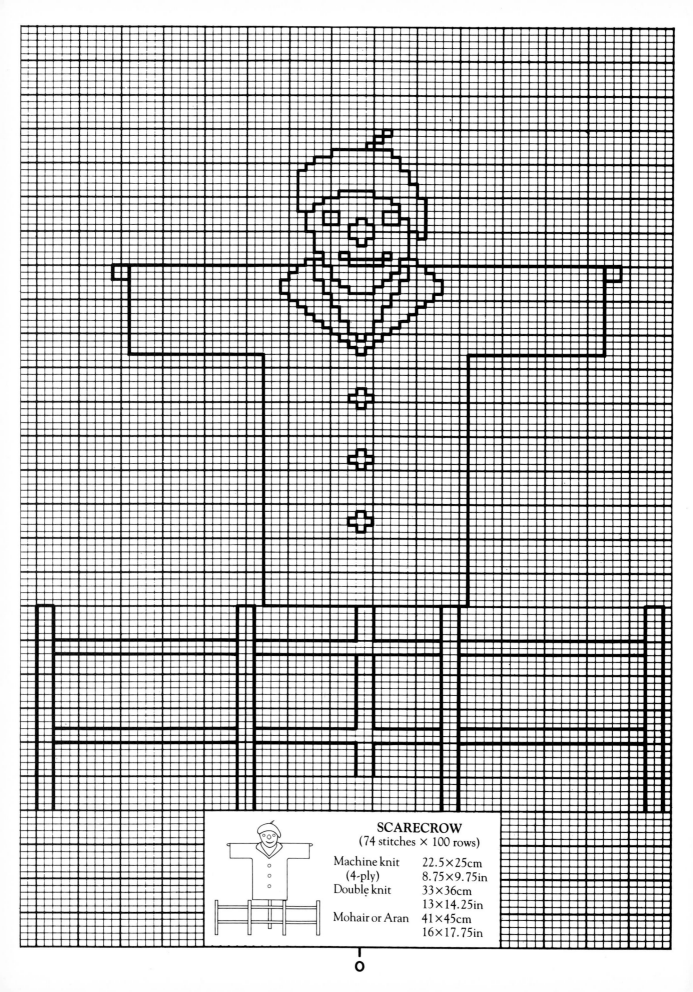

SCARECROW
(74 stitches × 100 rows)

Machine knit	22.5×25cm	
(4-ply)	8.75×9.75in	
Double knit	33×36cm	
	13×14.25in	
Mohair or Aran	41×45cm	
	16×17.75in	

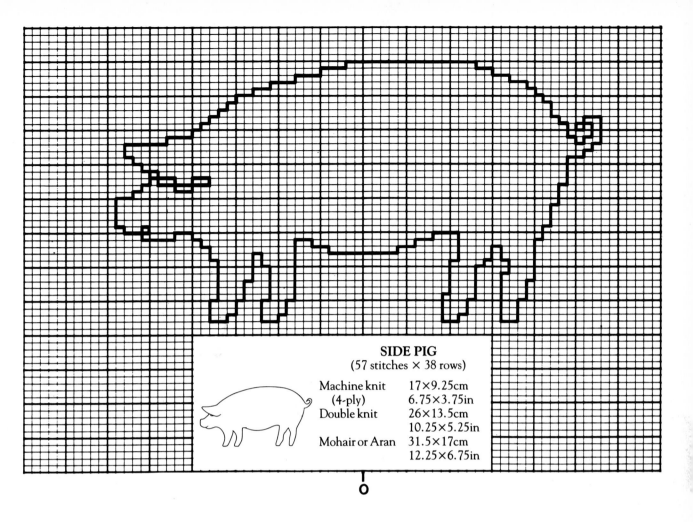

SIDE PIG
(57 stitches × 38 rows)

Machine knit	17×9.25cm	
(4-ply)	6.75×3.75in	
Double knit	26×13.5cm	
	10.25×5.25in	
Mohair or Aran	31.5×17cm	
	12.25×6.75in	

O

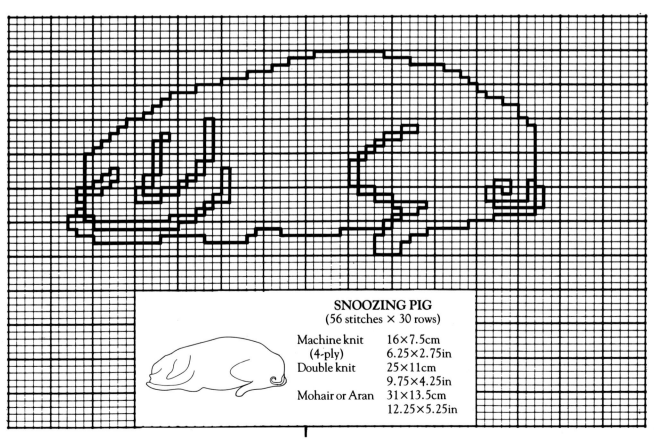

SNOOZING PIG
(56 stitches × 30 rows)

Machine knit	16×7.5cm	
(4-ply)	6.25×2.75in	
Double knit	25×11cm	
	9.75×4.25in	
Mohair or Aran	31×13.5cm	
	12.25×5.25in	

O

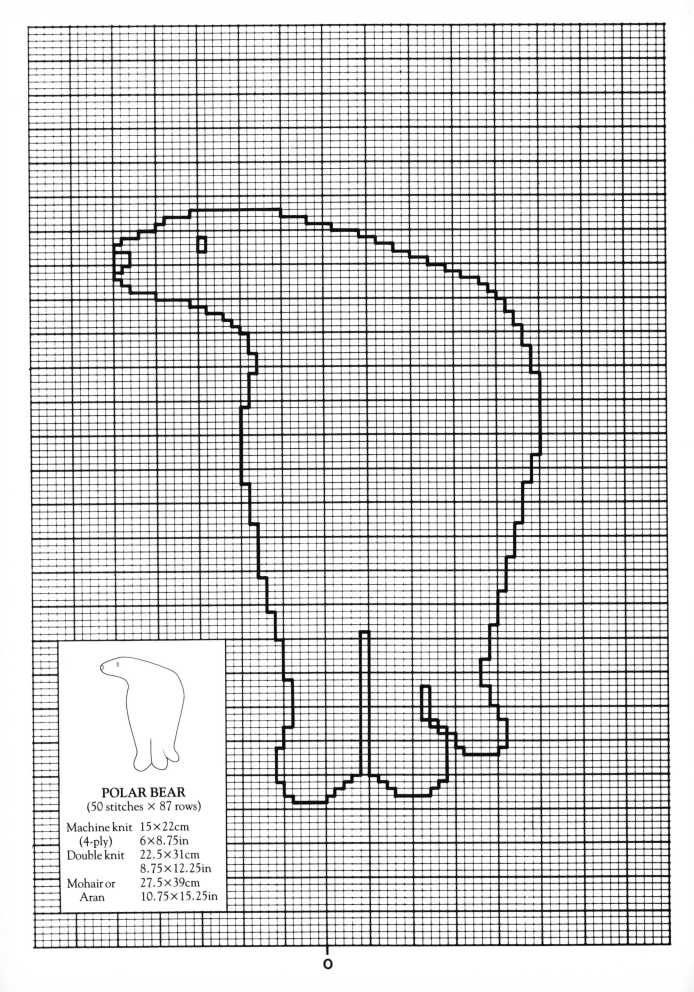

POLAR BEAR
(50 stitches × 87 rows)

Machine knit	15×22cm
(4-ply)	6×8.75in
Double knit	22.5×31cm
	8.75×12.25in
Mohair or	27.5×39cm
Aran	10.75×15.25in

O

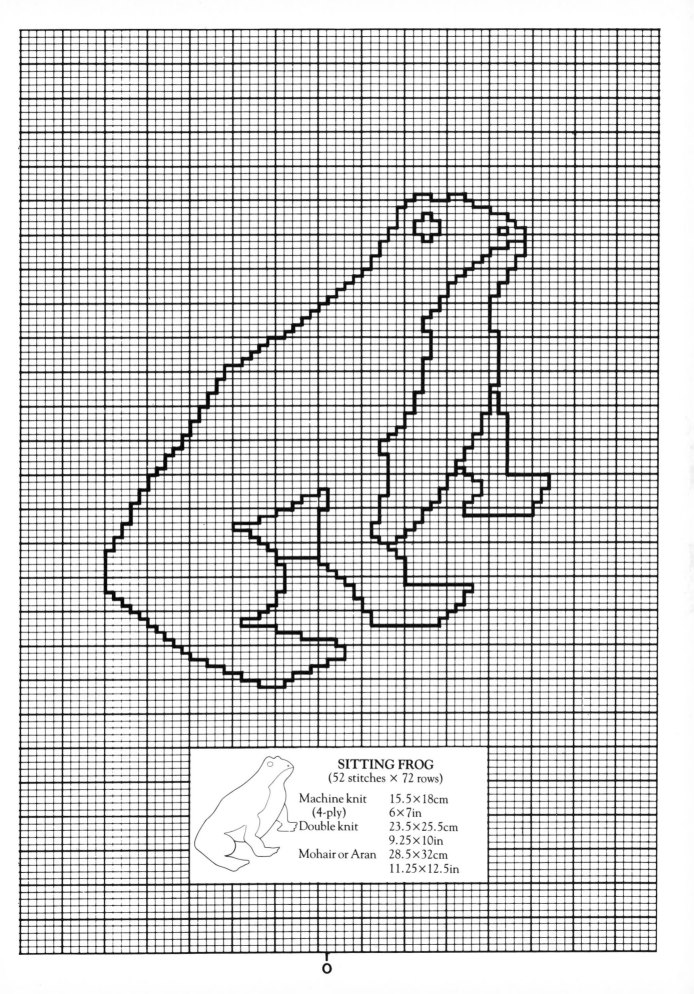

SITTING FROG
(52 stitches × 72 rows)

Machine knit	15.5×18cm
(4-ply)	6×7in
Double knit	23.5×25.5cm
	9.25×10in
Mohair or Aran	28.5×32cm
	11.25×12.5in

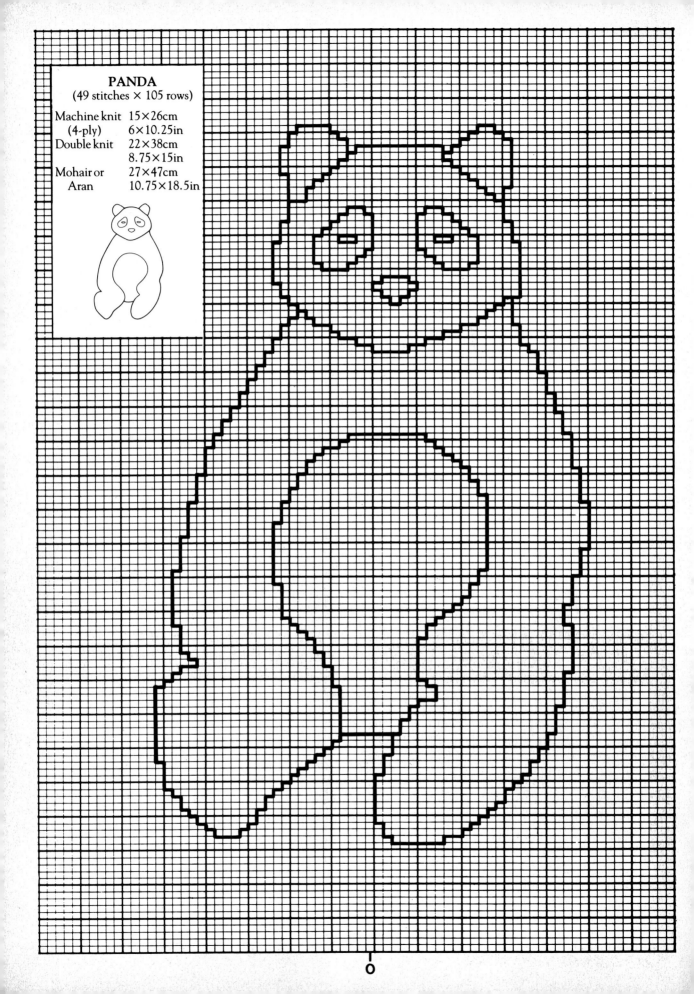

PANDA
(49 stitches × 105 rows)

Machine knit (4-ply)	15×26cm 6×10.25in
Double knit	22×38cm 8.75×15in
Mohair or Aran	27×47cm 10.75×18.5in

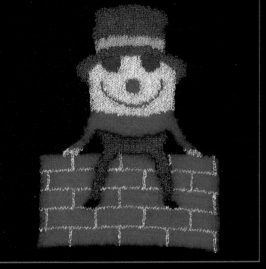

Humpty Dumpty (page 91)

Zebra (page 100)

Whale (page 79)

Squirrel (page 65)

Panda (page 76)

Koala Bear (page 90)

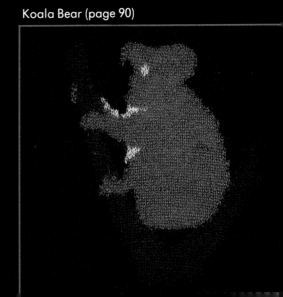

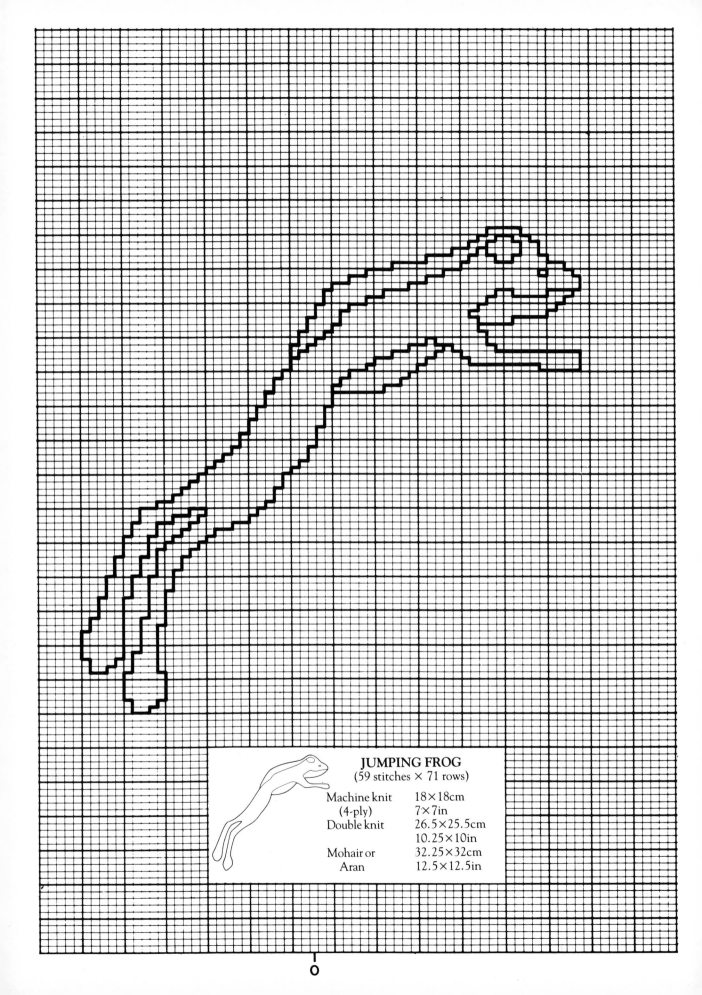

JUMPING FROG
(59 stitches × 71 rows)

Machine knit	18×18cm	
(4-ply)	7×7in	
Double knit	26.5×25.5cm	
	10.25×10in	
Mohair or	32.25×32cm	
Aran	12.5×12.5in	

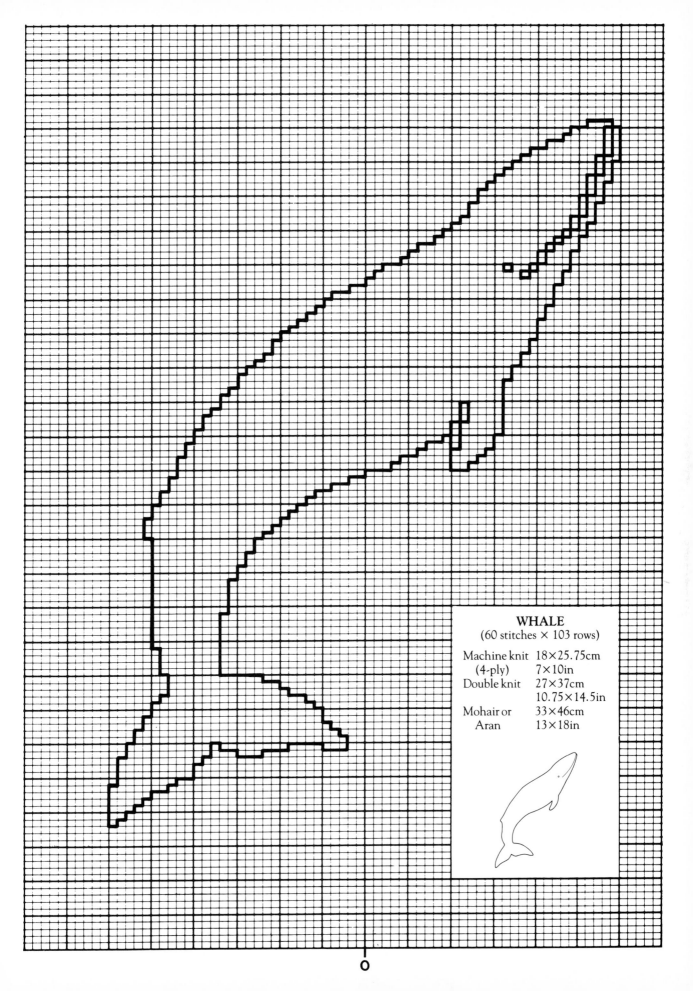

WHALE
(60 stitches × 103 rows)

Machine knit (4-ply)	18×25.75cm 7×10in
Double knit	27×37cm 10.75×14.5in
Mohair or Aran	33×46cm 13×18in

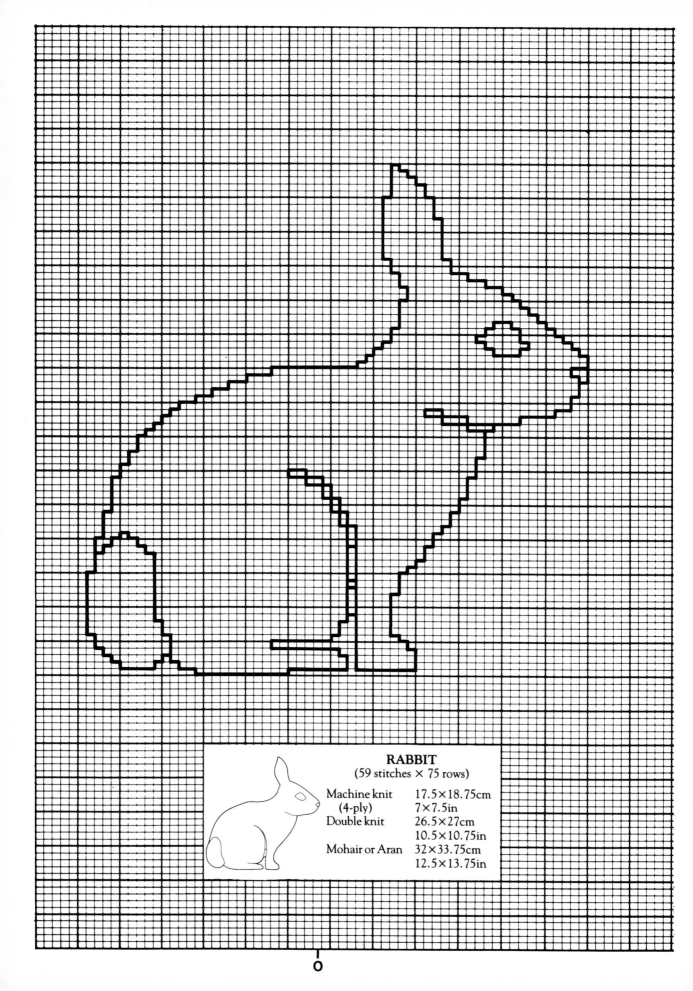

RABBIT
(59 stitches × 75 rows)

Machine knit	17.5×18.75cm	
(4-ply)	7×7.5in	
Double knit	26.5×27cm	
	10.5×10.75in	
Mohair or Aran	32×33.75cm	
	12.5×13.75in	

O

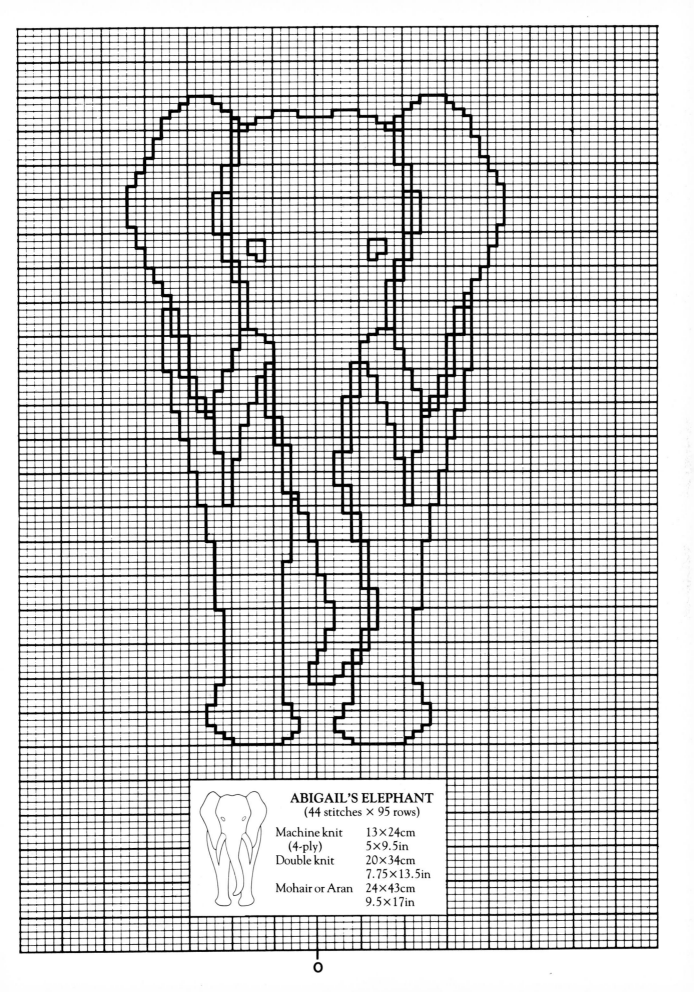

ABIGAIL'S ELEPHANT
(44 stitches × 95 rows)

Machine knit	13×24cm	
(4-ply)	5×9.5in	
Double knit	20×34cm	
	7.75×13.5in	
Mohair or Aran	24×43cm	
	9.5×17in	

O

DRESSED TEDDY FRONT
(55 stitches × 94 rows)

Machine knit	16.5×23.5cm	
(4-ply)	6.25×9.25in	
Double knit	25×34cm	
	9.75×13.5in	
Mohair or Aran	30.25×42cm	
	11.75×16.5in	

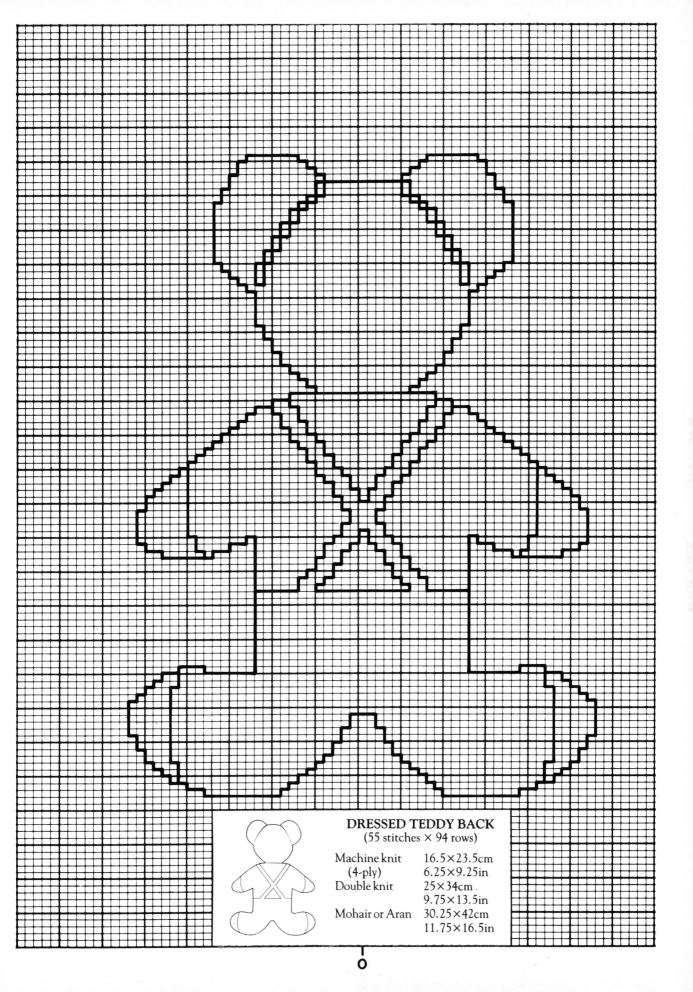

DRESSED TEDDY BACK
(55 stitches × 94 rows)

Machine knit	16.5×23.5cm	
(4-ply)	6.25×9.25in	
Double knit	25×34cm	
	9.75×13.5in	
Mohair or Aran	30.25×42cm	
	11.75×16.5in	

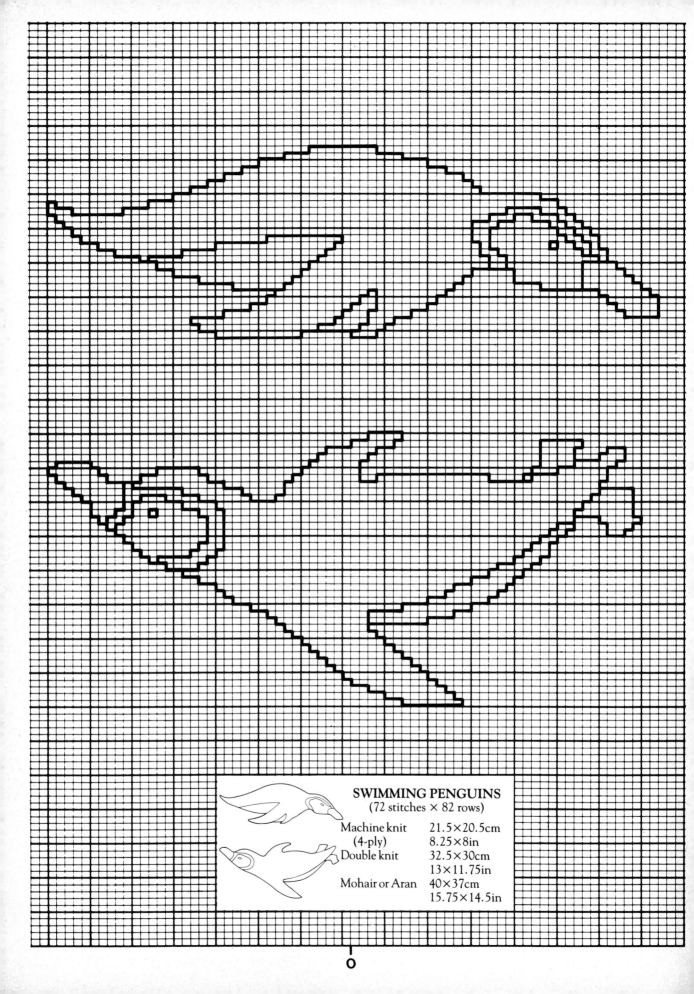

SWIMMING PENGUINS
(72 stitches × 82 rows)

Machine knit	21.5×20.5cm	
(4-ply)	8.25×8in	
Double knit	32.5×30cm	
	13×11.75in	
Mohair or Aran	40×37cm	
	15.75×14.5in	

O

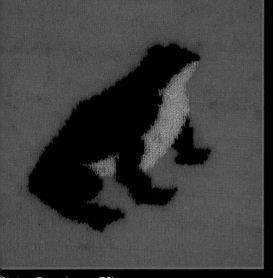

Sitting Frog (page 75)

Teddy Bear (page 44)

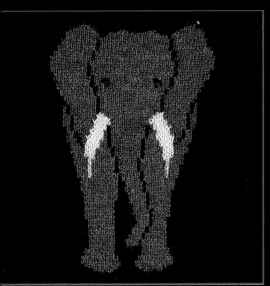

Abigail's Elephant (page 81)

Seal with Ball on Nose (page 86)

Badger (page 62)

Puffin (page 96)

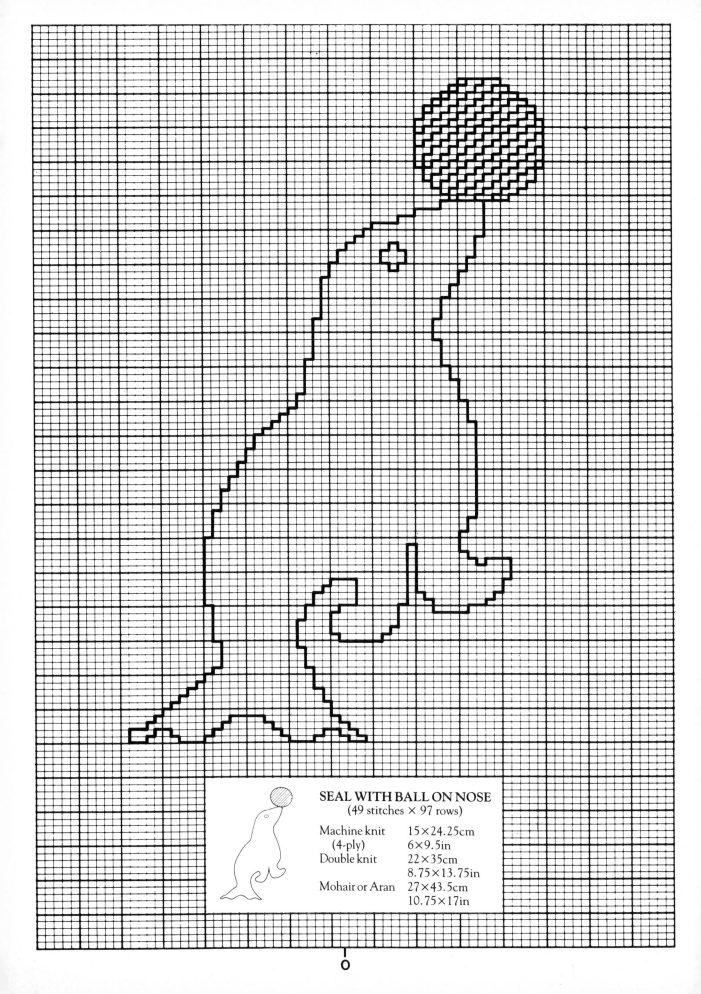

SEAL WITH BALL ON NOSE
(49 stitches × 97 rows)

Machine knit	15×24.25cm	
(4-ply)	6×9.5in	
Double knit	22×35cm	
	8.75×13.75in	
Mohair or Aran	27×43.5cm	
	10.75×17in	

O

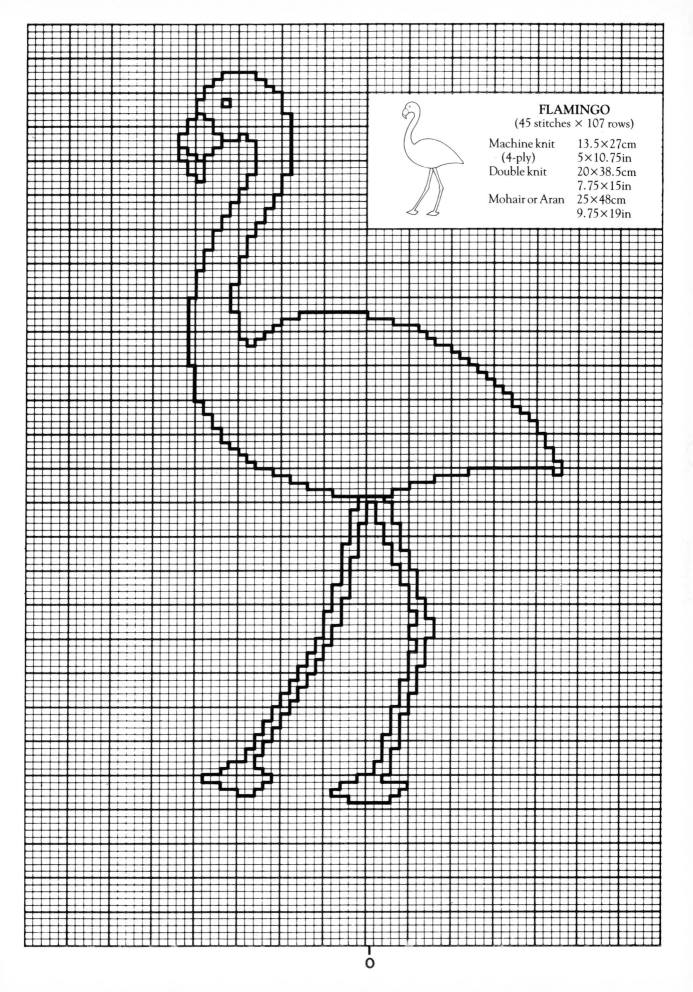

FLAMINGO
(45 stitches × 107 rows)

Machine knit	13.5×27cm	
(4-ply)	5×10.75in	
Double knit	20×38.5cm	
	7.75×15in	
Mohair or Aran	25×48cm	
	9.75×19in	

0

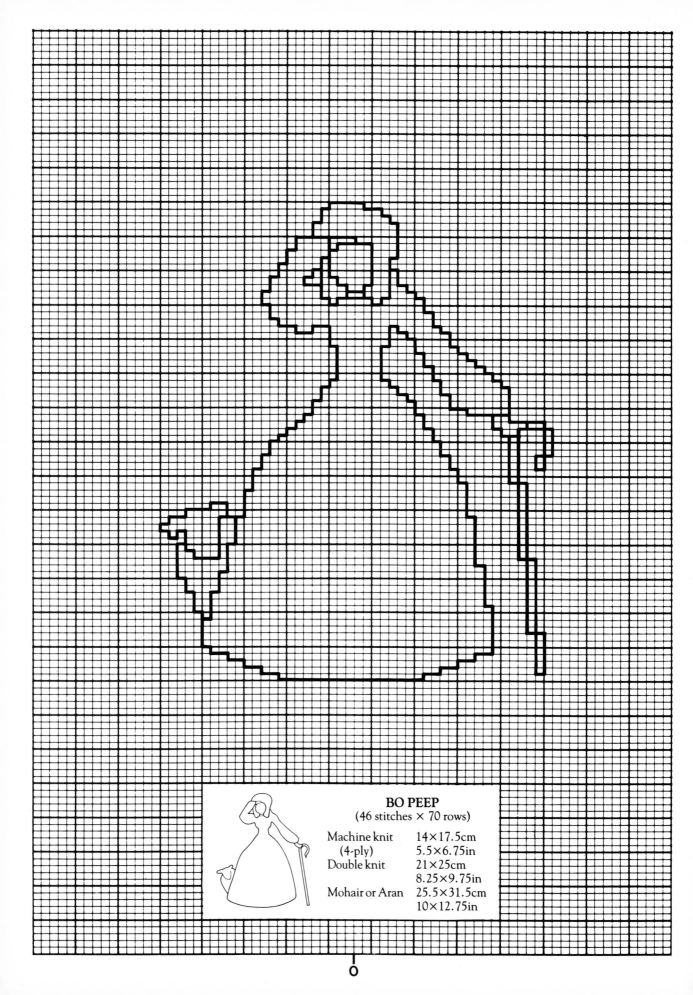

BO PEEP
(46 stitches × 70 rows)

Machine knit	14×17.5cm	
(4-ply)	5.5×6.75in	
Double knit	21×25cm	
	8.25×9.75in	
Mohair or Aran	25.5×31.5cm	
	10×12.75in	

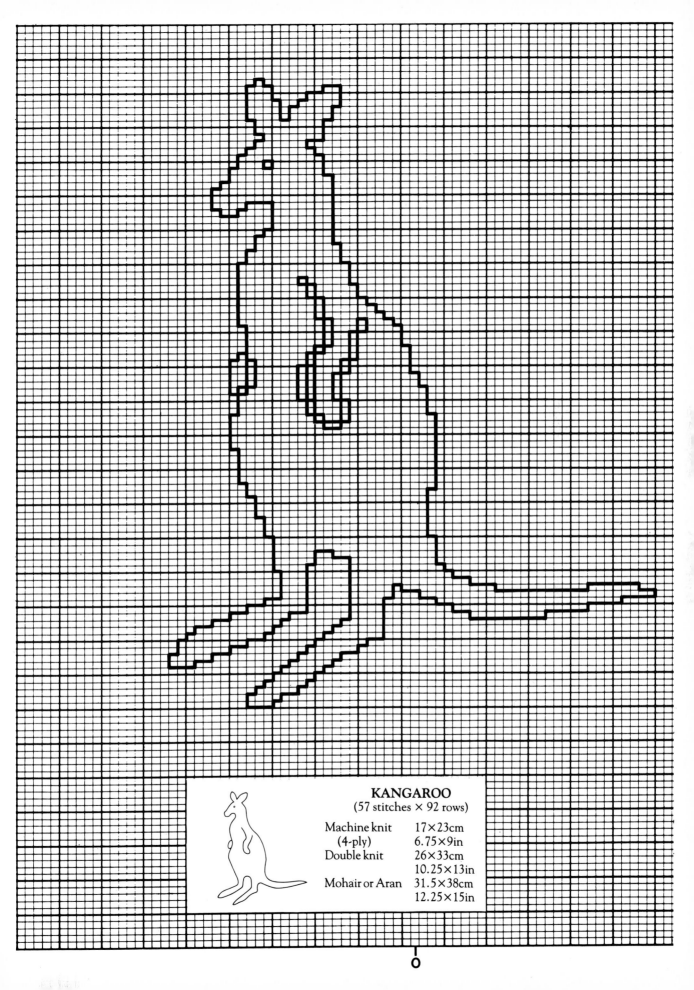

KANGAROO
(57 stitches × 92 rows)

Machine knit	17×23cm	
(4-ply)	6.75×9in	
Double knit	26×33cm	
	10.25×13in	
Mohair or Aran	31.5×38cm	
	12.25×15in	

0

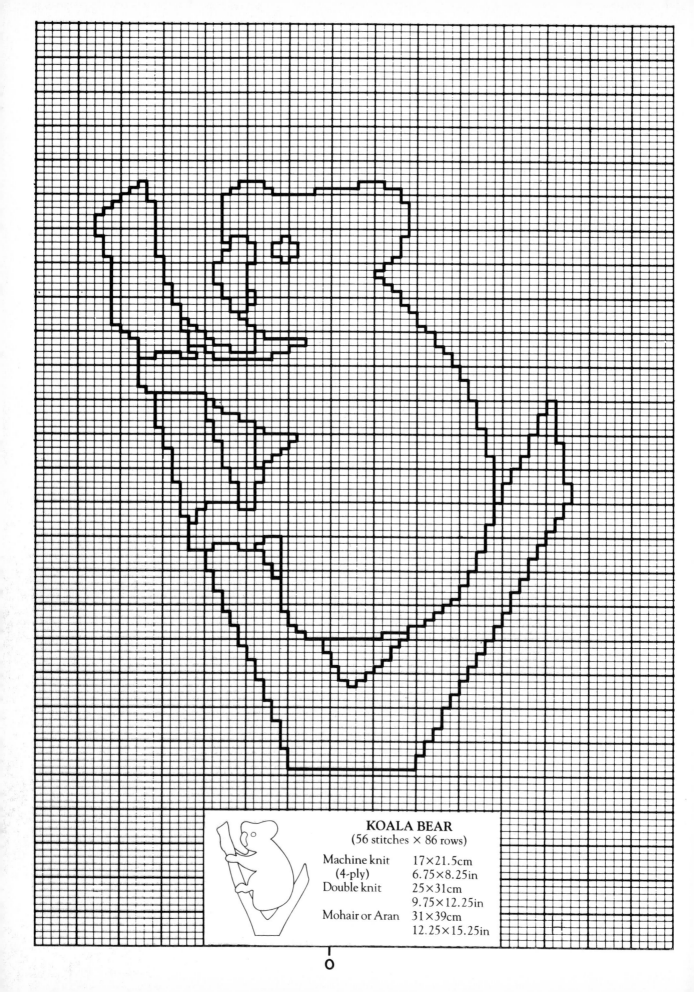

KOALA BEAR
(56 stitches × 86 rows)

Machine knit	17×21.5cm	
(4-ply)	6.75×8.25in	
Double knit	25×31cm	
	9.75×12.25in	
Mohair or Aran	31×39cm	
	12.25×15.25in	

HUMPTY DUMPTY
(60 stitches × 103 rows)

Machine knit	18×25.75cm	
(4-ply)	7×10in	
Double knit	27×37cm	
	10.75×14.5in	
Mohair or Aran	33×46cm	
	13×18in	

Man in the Moon (page 102)

Penguin (page 57)

Pheasant (page 99)

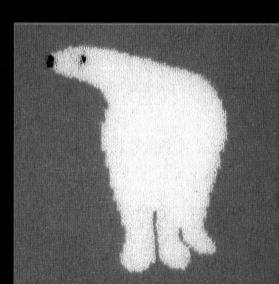

Polar Bear (page 74)

Reindeer (page 93)

Clown (page 97)

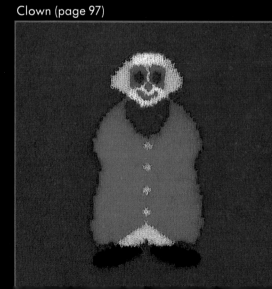

REINDEER
(54 stitches × 94 rows)

Machine knit	16×23.5cm	
(4-ply)	6.25×9.25in	
Double knit	24.5×34cm	
	9.5×13.5in	
Mohair or Aran	30×42cm	
	11.75×16.5in	

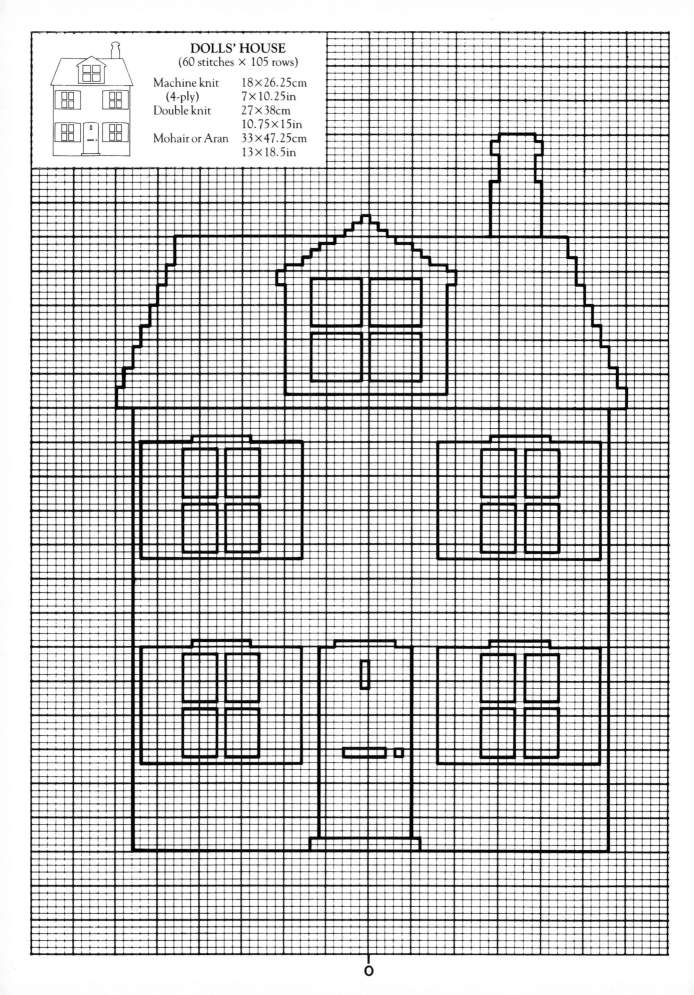

DOLLS' HOUSE
(60 stitches × 105 rows)

Machine knit	18×26.25cm
(4-ply)	7×10.25in
Double knit	27×38cm
	10.75×15in
Mohair or Aran	33×47.25cm
	13×18.5in

O

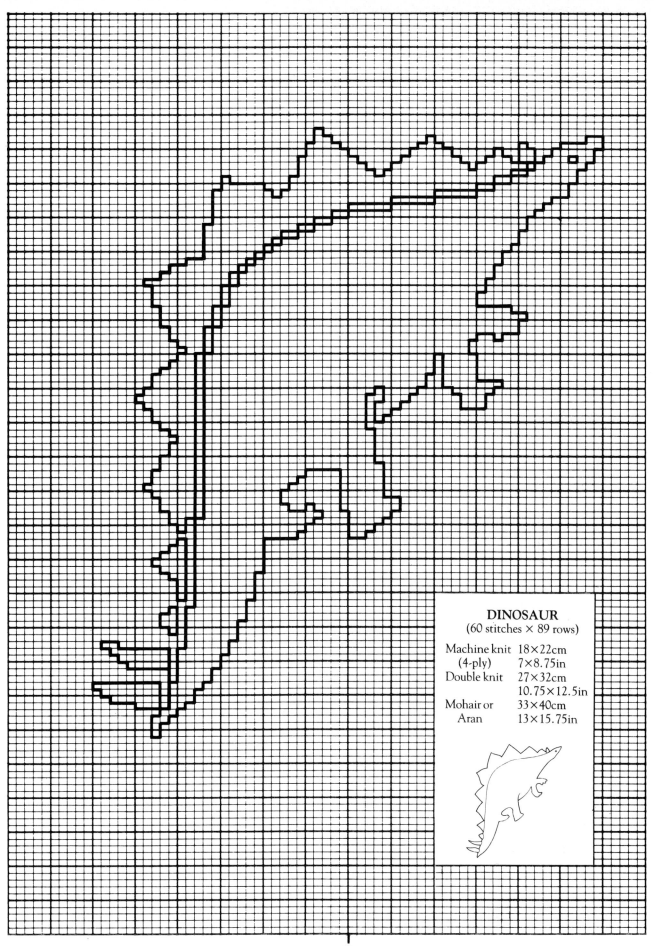

DINOSAUR
(60 stitches × 89 rows)

Machine knit	18×22cm
(4-ply)	7×8.75in
Double knit	27×32cm
	10.75×12.5in
Mohair or	33×40cm
Aran	13×15.75in

O

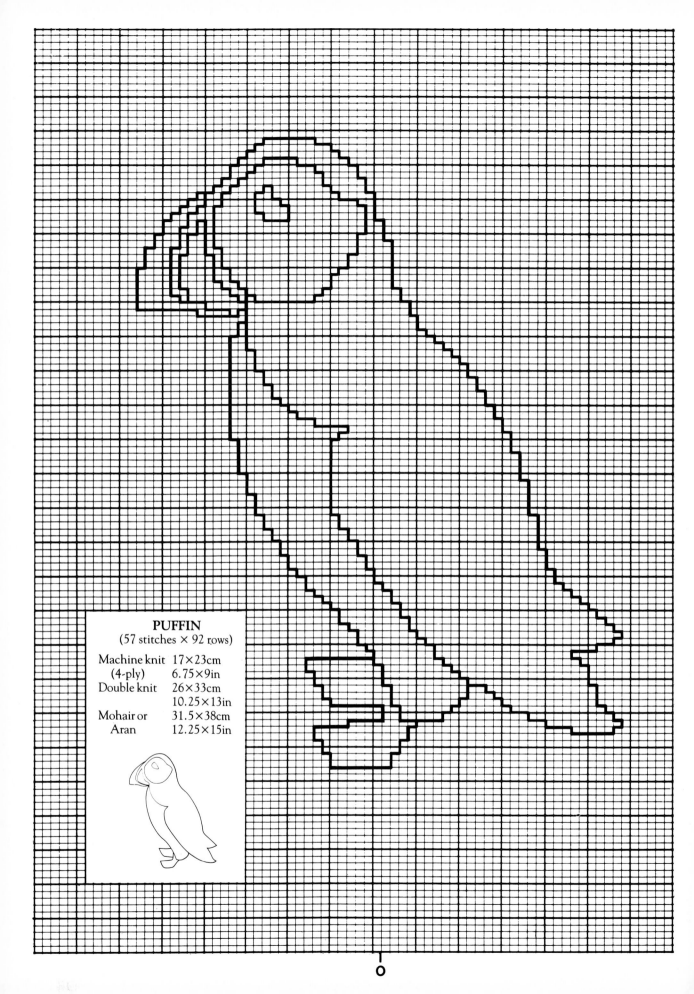

PUFFIN
(57 stitches × 92 rows)

Machine knit	17×23cm
(4-ply)	6.75×9in
Double knit	26×33cm
	10.25×13in
Mohair or	31.5×38cm
Aran	12.25×15in

o

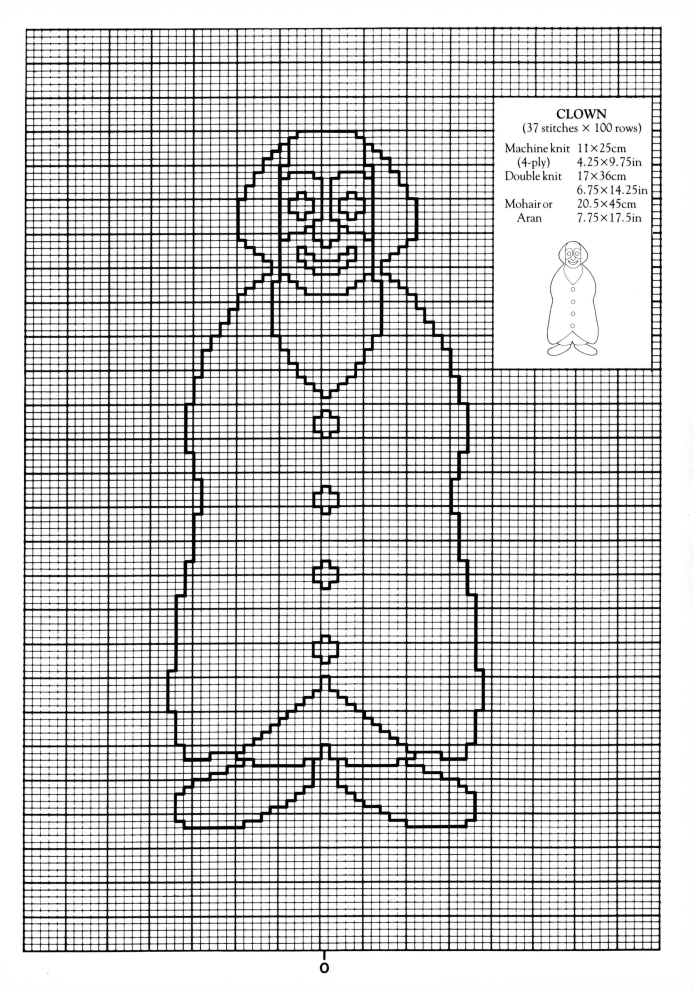

CLOWN
(37 stitches × 100 rows)

Machine knit (4-ply)	11×25cm	4.25×9.75in
Double knit	17×36cm	6.75×14.25in
Mohair or Aran	20.5×45cm	7.75×17.5in

ELEPHANT
(57 stitches × 100 rows)

Machine knit	17×25cm	
(4-ply)	6.75×9.75in	
Double knit	26×36cm	
	10.25×14.25in	
Mohair or Aran	31.5×45cm	
	12.25×17.75in	

O

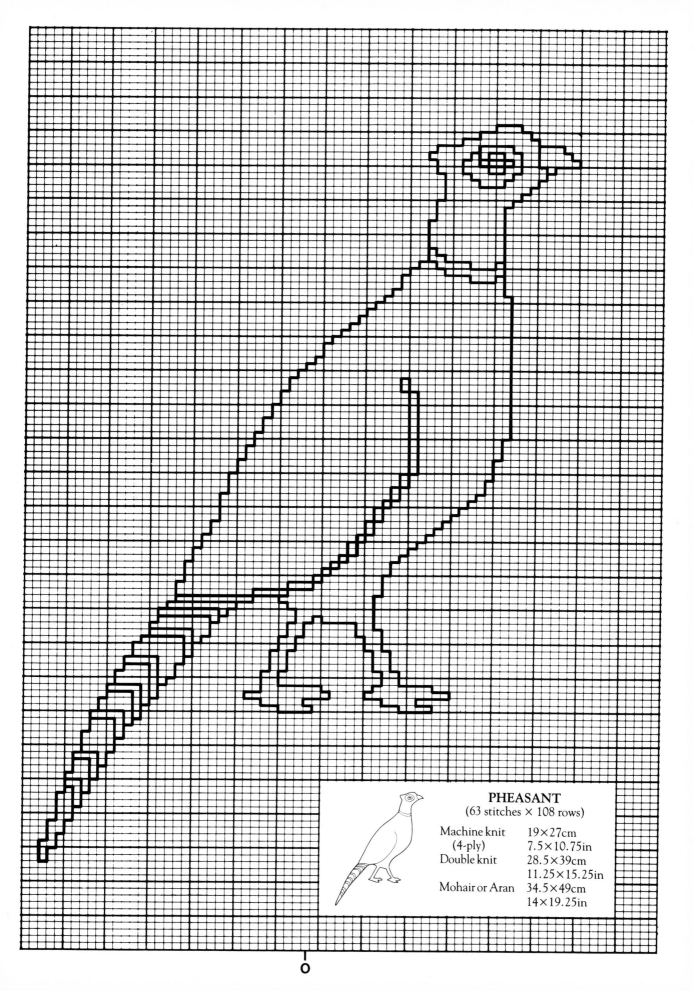

PHEASANT
(63 stitches × 108 rows)

Machine knit	19×27cm	
(4-ply)	7.5×10.75in	
Double knit	28.5×39cm	
	11.25×15.25in	
Mohair or Aran	34.5×49cm	
	14×19.25in	

O

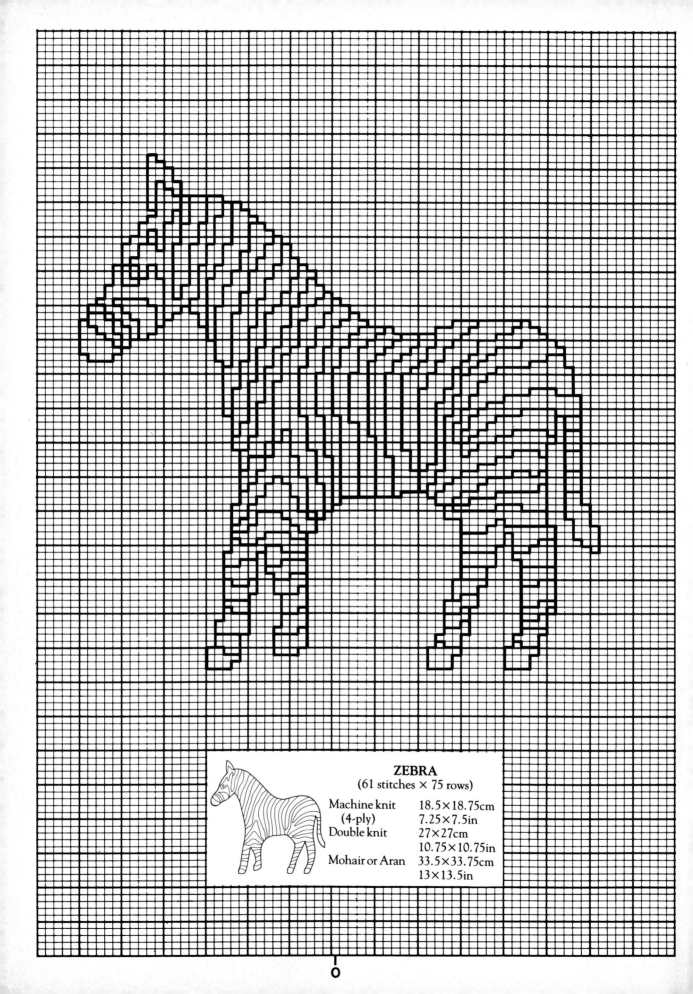

ZEBRA
(61 stitches × 75 rows)

Machine knit	18.5×18.75cm	
(4-ply)	7.25×7.5in	
Double knit	27×27cm	
	10.75×10.75in	
Mohair or Aran	33.5×33.75cm	
	13×13.5in	

O

Pig on the Wall (page 67)

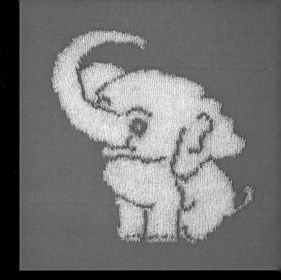

Elephant (page 98)

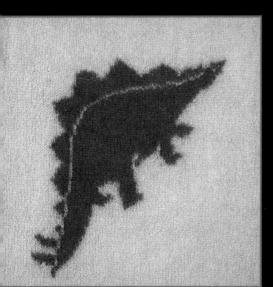

Dinosaur (page 95)

Sitting Dog (page 58)

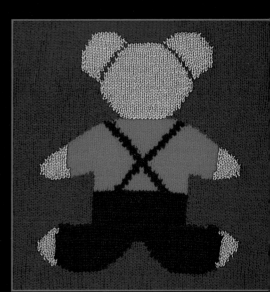

Dressed Teddy Back (page 83)

Giraffe (page 104)

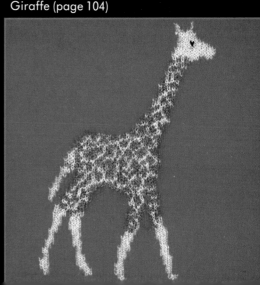

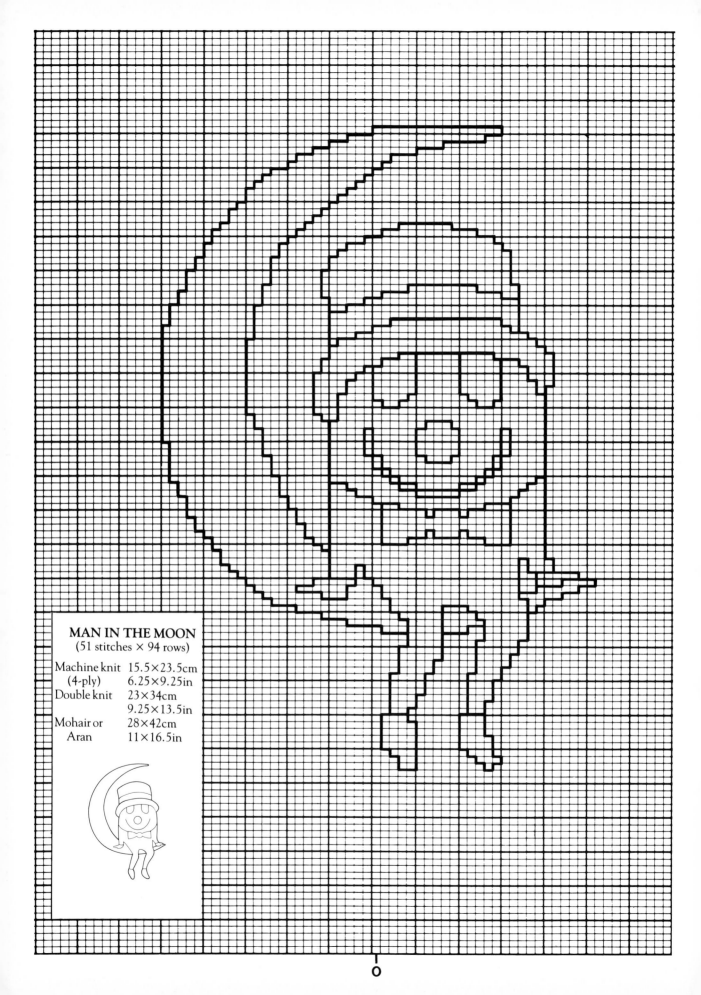

MAN IN THE MOON
(51 stitches × 94 rows)

Machine knit (4-ply)	15.5×23.5cm	6.25×9.25in
Double knit	23×34cm	9.25×13.5in
Mohair or Aran	28×42cm	11×16.5in

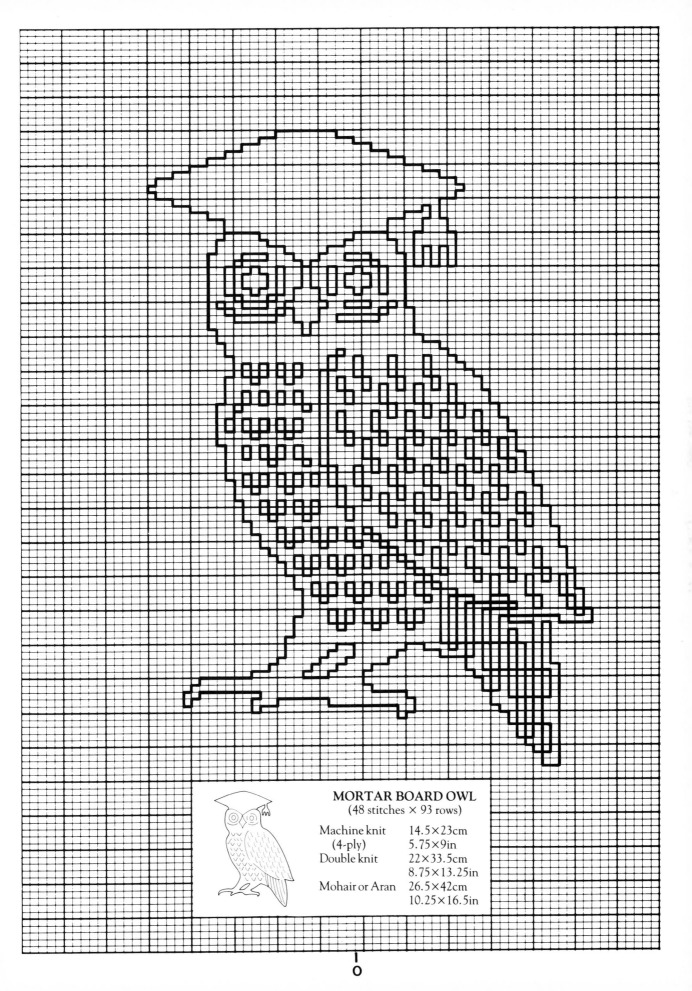

MORTAR BOARD OWL
(48 stitches × 93 rows)

Machine knit	14.5×23cm	
(4-ply)	5.75×9in	
Double knit	22×33.5cm	
	8.75×13.25in	
Mohair or Aran	26.5×42cm	
	10.25×16.5in	

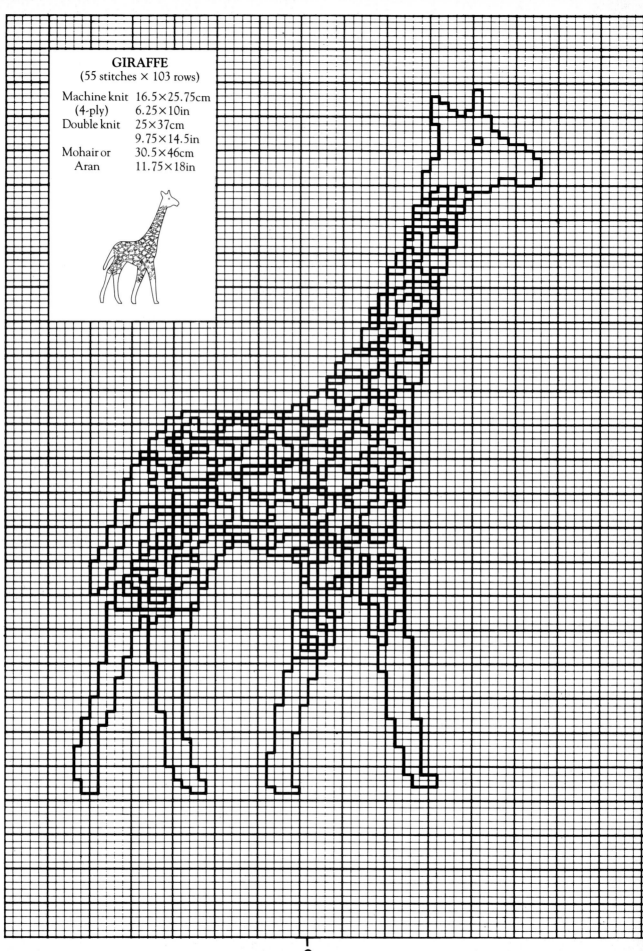

GIRAFFE
(55 stitches × 103 rows)

Machine knit (4-ply)	16.5×25.75cm 6.25×10in
Double knit	25×37cm 9.75×14.5in
Mohair or Aran	30.5×46cm 11.75×18in

O

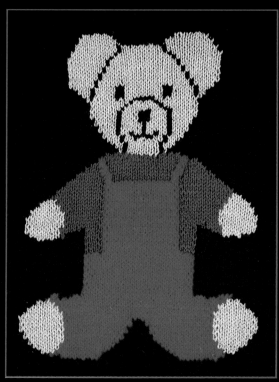

Dressed Teddy Front (page 82)

Teddy in Stocking (page 110)

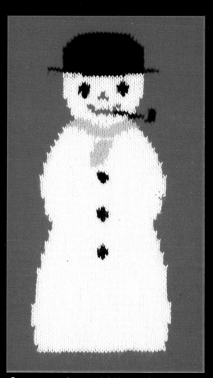

Snowman (page 108)

Seal with Ball on Tail (page 106)

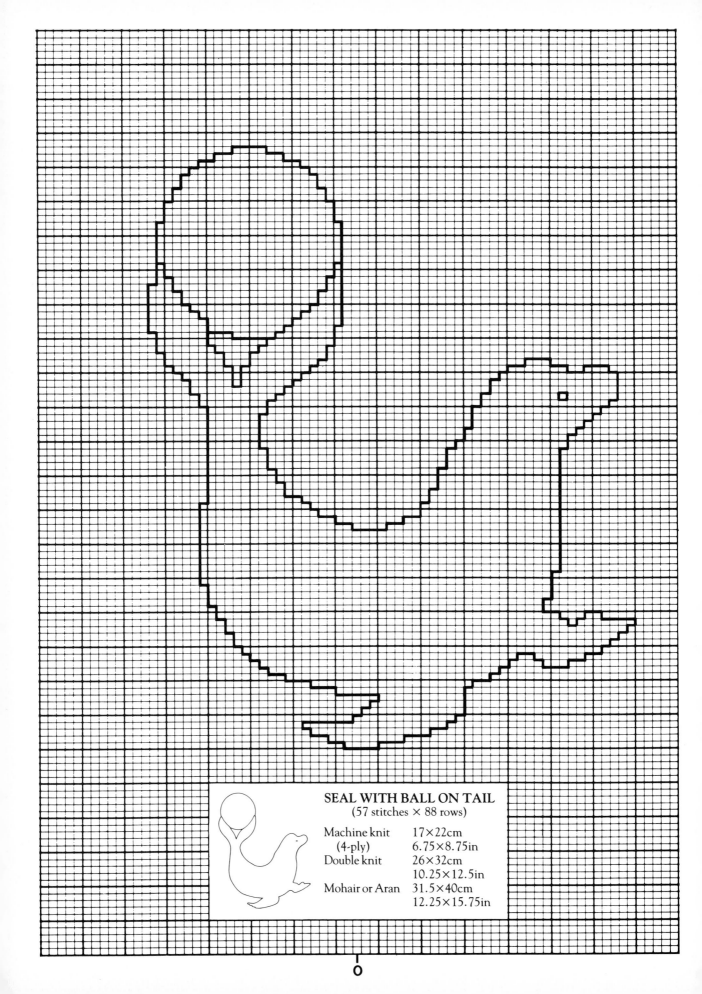

SEAL WITH BALL ON TAIL
(57 stitches × 88 rows)

Machine knit	17×22cm
(4-ply)	6.75×8.75in
Double knit	26×32cm
	10.25×12.5in
Mohair or Aran	31.5×40cm
	12.25×15.75in

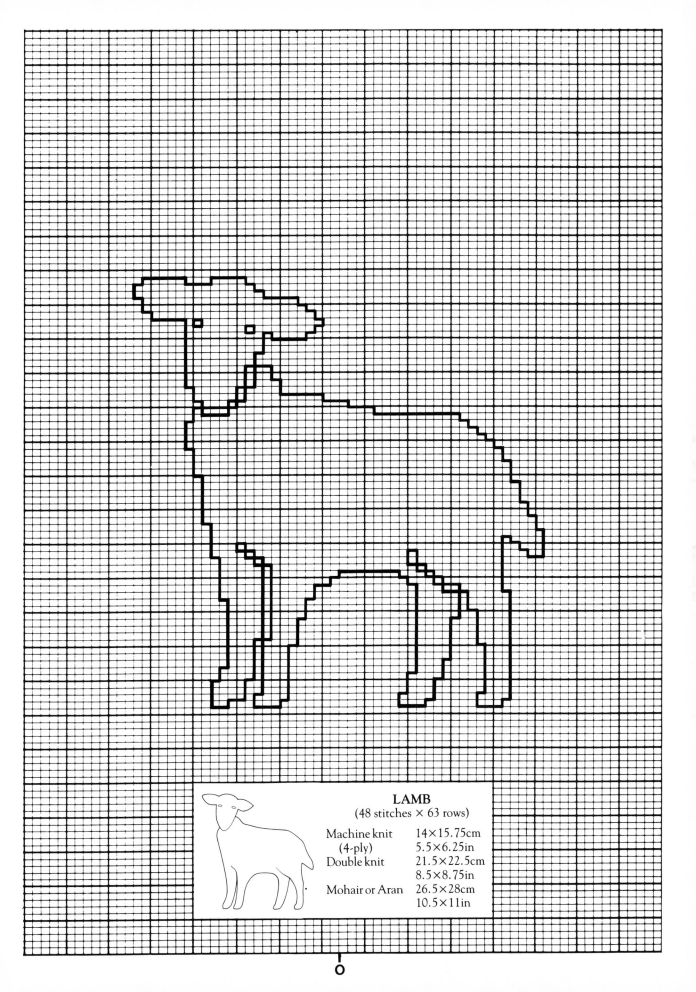

LAMB
(48 stitches × 63 rows)

Machine knit	14×15.75cm
(4-ply)	5.5×6.25in
Double knit	21.5×22.5cm
	8.5×8.75in
Mohair or Aran	26.5×28cm
	10.5×11in

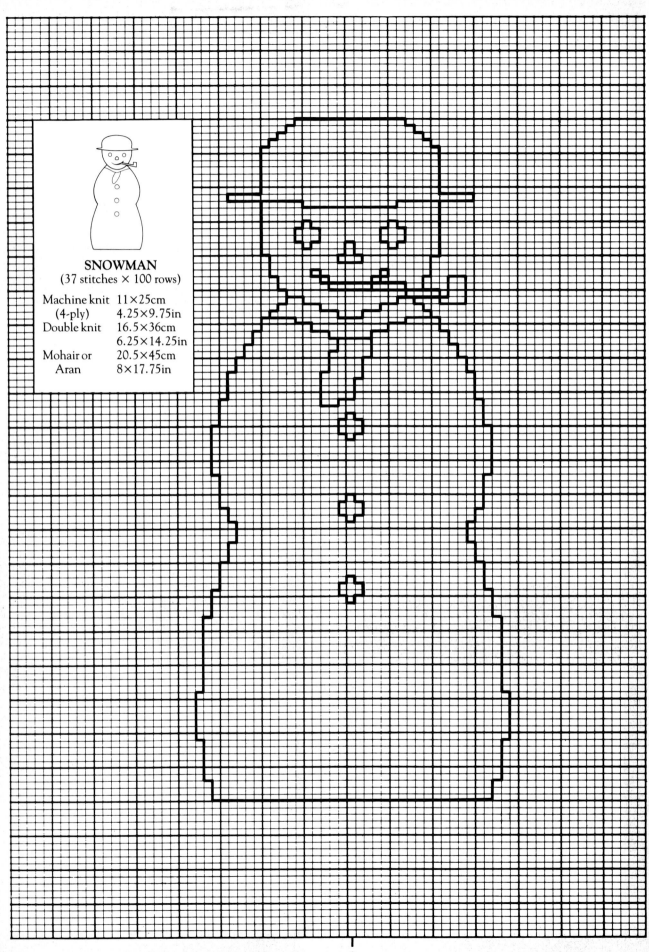

SNOWMAN
(37 stitches × 100 rows)

Machine knit (4-ply)	11×25cm 4.25×9.75in
Double knit	16.5×36cm 6.25×14.25in
Mohair or Aran	20.5×45cm 8×17.75in

Small Mouse (page 114)

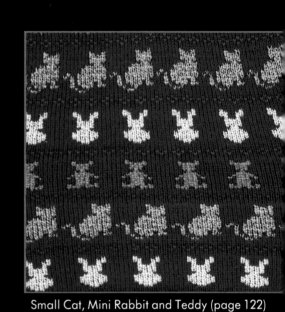

Small Standing Teddy (page 119)

Small Penguin (page 115)

Small Cat, Mini Rabbit and Teddy (page 122)

Small Cat and Snail (page 114)

Tiny Teddy (page 119)

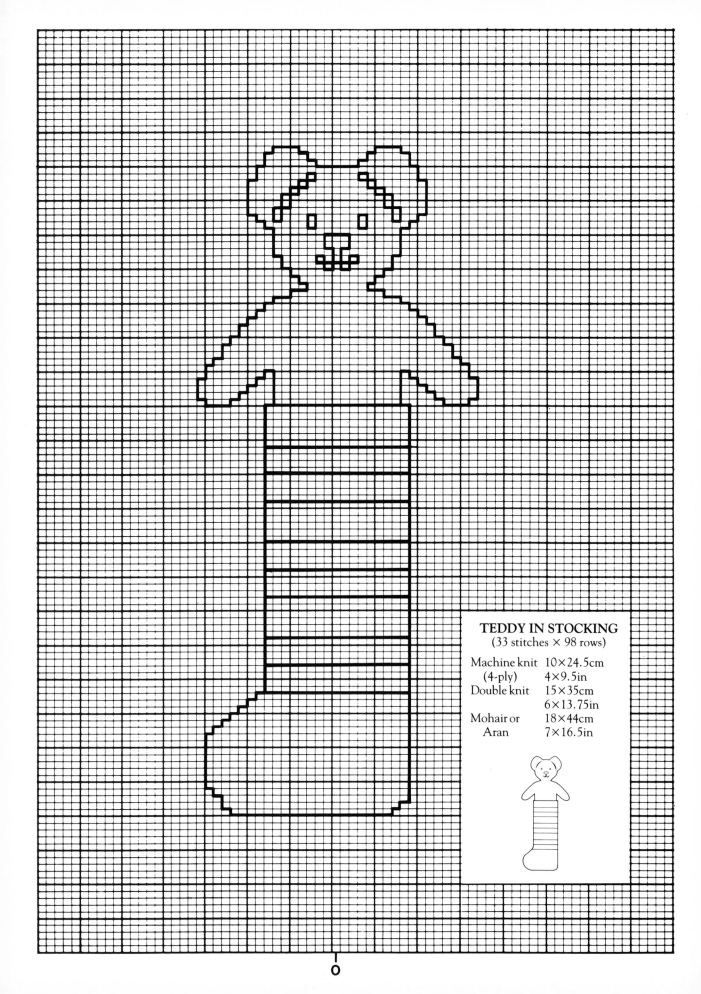

TEDDY IN STOCKING
(33 stitches × 98 rows)

Machine knit	10×24.5cm	
(4-ply)	4×9.5in	
Double knit	15×35cm	
	6×13.75in	
Mohair or	18×44cm	
Aran	7×16.5in	

o

SCATTERED MOTIFS

Working with scattered motifs provides the knitter with endless opportunities to create unique and individual designs. Above all, it is fun. Try placing a large motif together with smaller versions. For instance you can create a whole family of rabbits with Mum surrounded by babies and junior rabbits, or a whole flock of Puffins, or as many Teddies as you like. The two basic dropped-shoulder patterns are easy to work with as you are not restricted when it comes to the positioning of the motifs.

Naturally, it is much easier if you are only knitting one motif because you only have to think about one pattern block at a time, but don't be put off; thinking about several designs at once is not as difficult as you might think. Use the design paper that has been provided at the end of this book to help you work out your own layout, then it is simply a case of following your own design. Machine knitters will find that they will need to think carefully about placing the motifs in order to avoid over-long floats between the individual motifs.

Name	Stitches	Rows
Small Duck	16	30
Small Seal	20	37
Small Mouse	22	24
Small Snail	22	22
Small Cat	18	22
Small Rabbit	15	24
Large Duck	23	48
Large Rabbit	20	46
Small Penguin	19	49
Small Panda	24	50
Small Lion	23	40
Small Owl	19	50
Small Frog	29	38
Small Dinosaur	30	43
Elephant (Big Ears)	39	47
Small Elephant	26	42
Tiny Teddy	23	32
Small Standing Teddy	21	40
Sitting Teddy	33	48

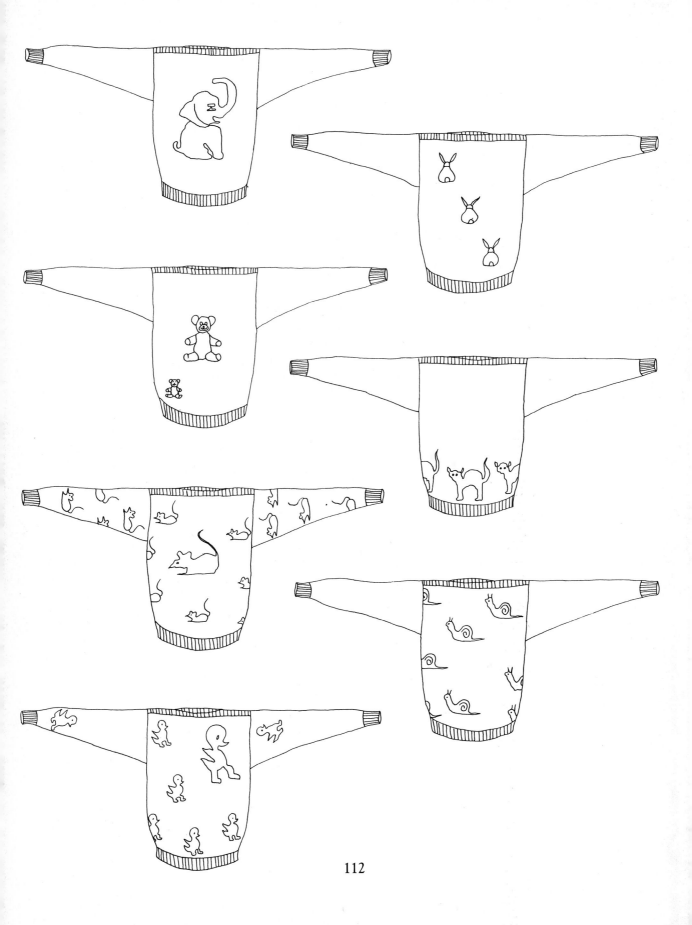

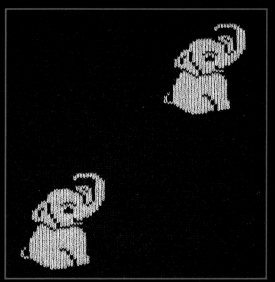

Small Elephant (page 118)

Sitting Teddy (page 119)

Small Owl (page 116)

Large Duck (page 115)

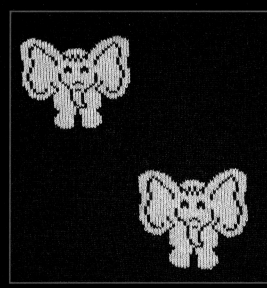

Elephant Big Ears (page 118)

Large Rabbit (page 115)

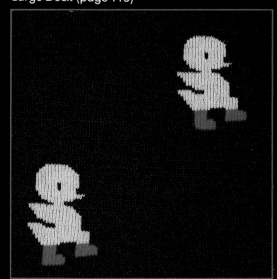

SMALL DUCK (16sts × 30 rows)

Machine knit (4-ply)	5×6.5cm	2×2.5in
Double knit	7×11cm	2.75×4.25in
Mohair or Aran	9×13.5cm	3.5×5in

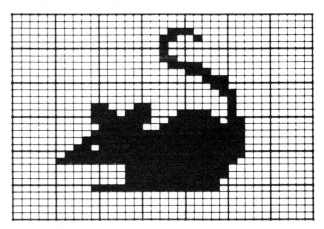

SMALL MOUSE (22sts × 24 rows)

Machine knit (4-ply)	6.5×6cm	2.5×2.25in
Double knit	10×8.5cm	4×3.5in
Mohair or Aran	12×11cm	4.75×4.25in

SMALL SNAIL (22sts × 22 rows)

Machine knit (4-ply)	6.5×5.5cm	2.5×2in
Double knit	10×8cm	4×3.25in
Mohair or Aran	12×10cm	4.75×4in

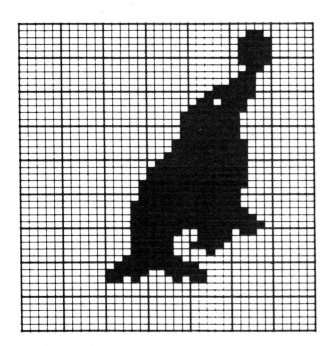

SMALL SEAL (20sts × 37 rows)

Machine knit (4-ply)	5.5×9cm	2×3.5in
Double knit	8.5×13cm	3.25×5in
Mohair or Aran	10.5×16.5cm	4×6.25in

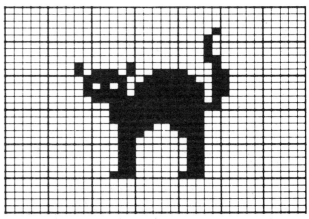

SMALL CAT (18sts × 22 rows)

Machine knit (4-ply)	5.5×5.5cm	2×2in
Double knit	8×8cm	3.25×3.25in
Mohair or Aran	10×10cm	4×4in

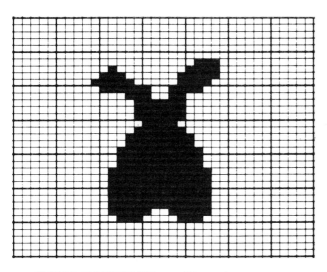

SMALL RABBIT (15sts × 24 rows)

Machine knit (4-ply)	5×6cm	1.75×2.25in
Double knit	7×8.5cm	2.75×3.25in
Mohair or Aran	9×11cm	3.5×4.25in

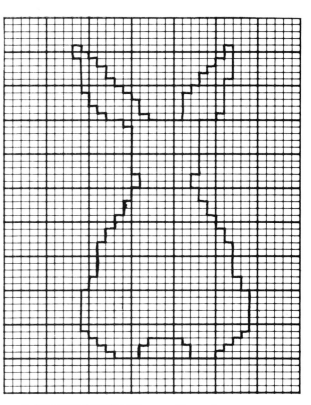

LARGE RABBIT (20sts × 46 rows)

Machine knit (4-ply)	6×11.5cm	2.25×4.25in
Double knit	9×16.5cm	3.5×6.5in
Mohair or Aran	11×21cm	4.25×8.25in

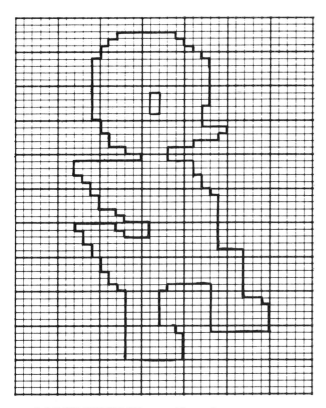

LARGE DUCK (23sts × 48 rows)

Machine knit (4-ply)	7×12cm	2.75×4.75in
Double knit	10×17cm	4×6.75in
Mohair or Aran	12.5×20cm	4.75×7.75in

SMALL PENGUIN (19sts × 49 rows)

Machine knit (4-ply)	5.5×12cm	2×4.75in
Double knit	8.5×17.5cm	3.25×6.75in
Mohair or Aran	10.5×22cm	4×8.75in

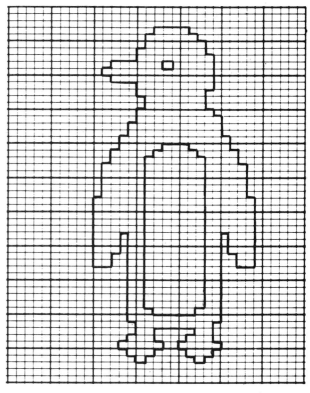

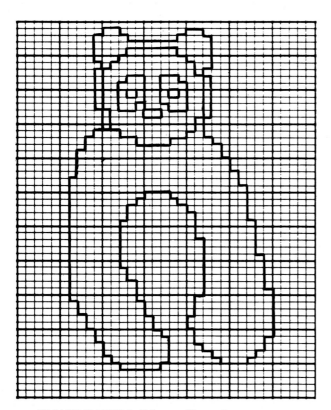

SMALL PANDA (24sts × 50 rows)

Machine knit (4-ply)	7×12.5cm	2.75×4.75in
Double knit	11×18cm	4.25×7in
Mohair or Aran	13×22.5cm	5×8.75in

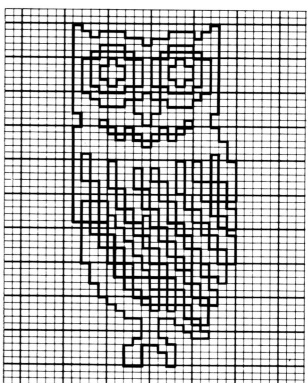

SMALL OWL (21sts × 38 rows)

Machine knit (4-ply)	5.5×12.5cm	2×4.75in
Double knit	8.5×18cm	4.25×7in
Mohair or Aran	10.5×22.5cm	5×8.5in

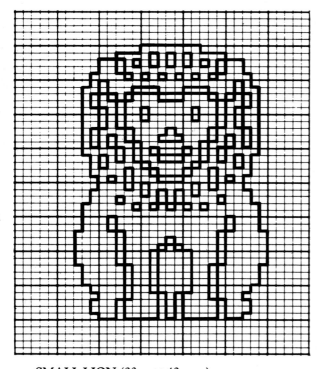

SMALL LION (23sts × 40 rows)

Machine knit (4-ply)	7×10cm	2.75×4in
Double knit	10.5×14.5cm	4×5.5in
Mohair or Aran	13×18cm	5×7in

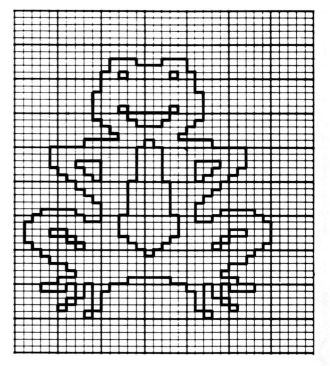

SMALL FROG (29sts × 38 rows)

Machine knit (4-ply)	9×9cm	3.5×3.5in
Double knit	13×13cm	5×5in
Mohair or Aran	16×16.5cm	6.25×6.25in

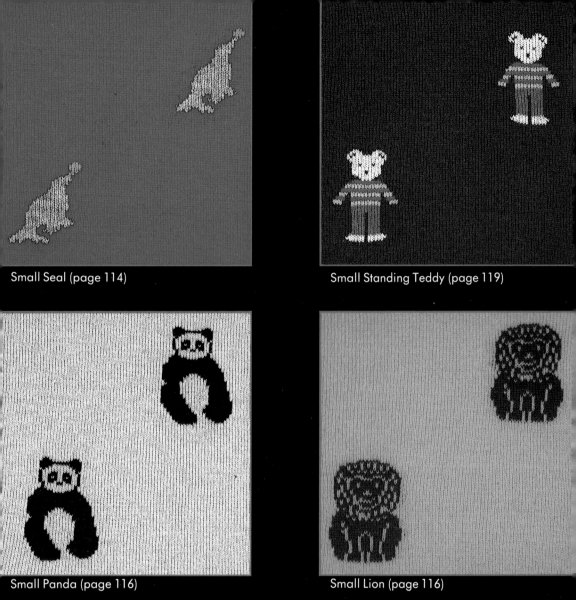

Small Seal (page 114)

Small Standing Teddy (page 119)

Small Panda (page 116)

Small Dinosaur (page 118)

Small Lion (page 116)

Small Frog (page 116)

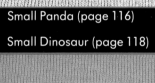

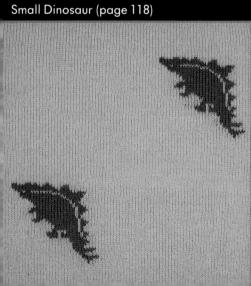

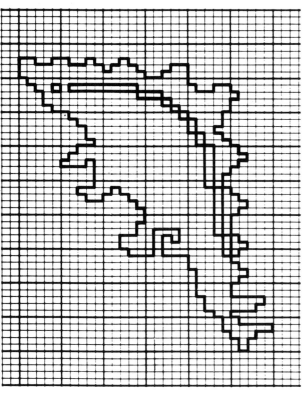

SMALL DINOSAUR (30sts × 43 rows)

Machine knit (4-ply)	9×11cm	3.5×4.25in
Double knit	13.5×15.5cm	5.25×6in
Mohair or Aran	16.5×23.5cm	6.25×9in

SMALL ELEPHANT (26sts × 42 rows)

Machine knit (4-ply)	8×10.5cm	3.25×4in
Double knit	11.5×15cm	4.25×6in
Mohair or Aran	14×19cm	5.5×7.5in

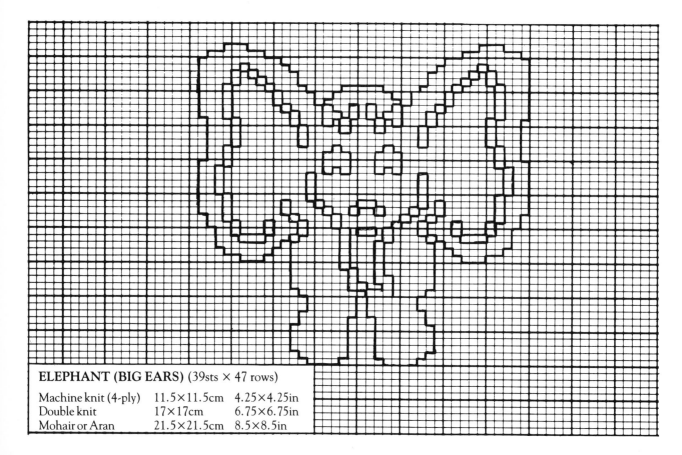

ELEPHANT (BIG EARS) (39sts × 47 rows)

Machine knit (4-ply)	11.5×11.5cm	4.25×4.25in
Double knit	17×17cm	6.75×6.75in
Mohair or Aran	21.5×21.5cm	8.5×8.5in

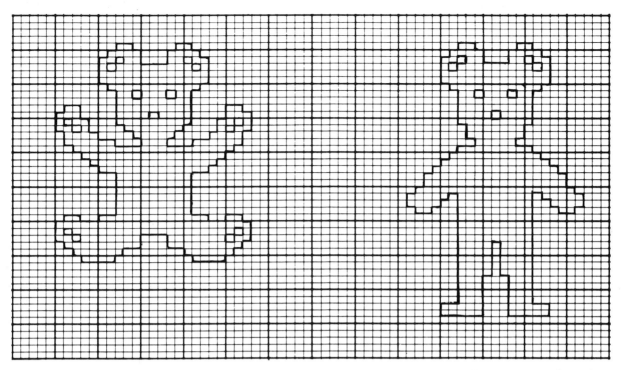

TINY TEDDY (23sts × 32 rows)

Machine knit (4-ply)	7×8cm	2.75×3.25in
Double knit	10.5×11.5cm	4×4.25in
Mohair or Aran	12.5×14.5cm	4.75×5.5in

SMALL STANDING TEDDY (21sts × 40 rows)

Machine knit (4-ply)	6×10cm	2.25×4in
Double knit	9.5×14.5cm	3.25×5.5in
Mohair or Aran	11.5×18cm	4.25×7in

SITTING TEDDY (33sts × 48 rows)

Machine knit (4-ply)	10×12cm	4×4.75in
Double knit	15×17cm	6×6.75in
Mohair or Aran	18×21.5cm	7×8.25in

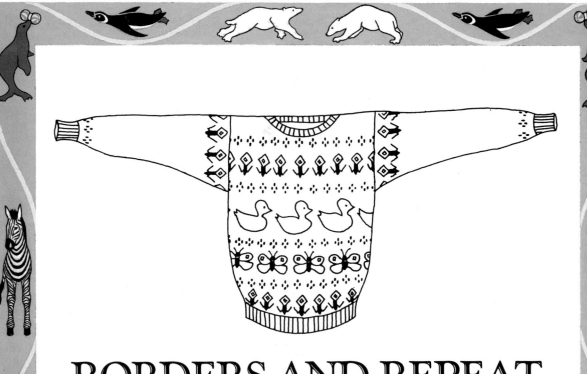

BORDERS AND REPEAT PATTERNS

Fair Isle and other repeat patterns can be used either to form the whole garment or just to provide interest to the cuffs and ribbing. These repeat patterns are very easy to place and can be used in combination with each other to make up your Fair Isle styled garment. Alternatively, try a combination of borders, repeats and scattered motifs. An example is shown above.

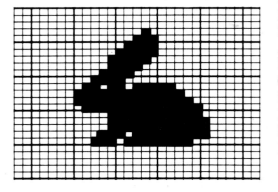

Name	Stitches	Rows
Rabbit	16	17
Hedgehog	10	8
Owl	7	14
Cat	11	15
Squirrel	10	14
Duck	11	14
Mini Rabbit	6	14
Flower	9	10
House	11	10
Butterfly	11	8
Apple Tree	8	12
Fir Tree	11	18
Church	11	13
Mini Teddy	7	12
Boy and Girl	24	15
Fair Isle repeat pattern		
Border patterns		

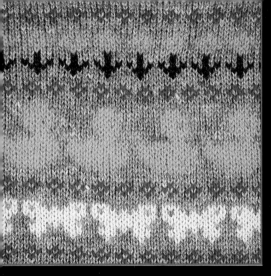
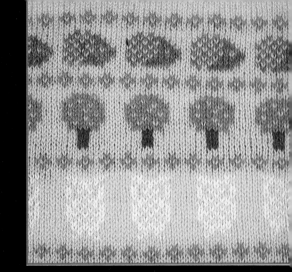

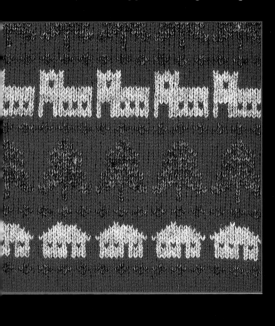

Suggested designs using borders and repeat patterns (pages 122 & 126)

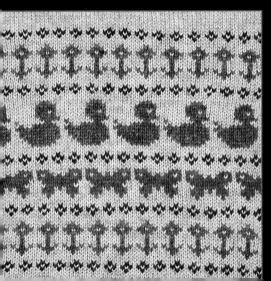
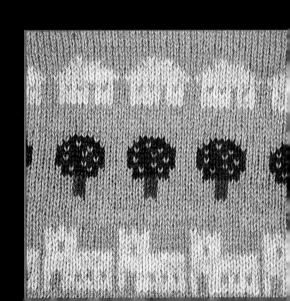

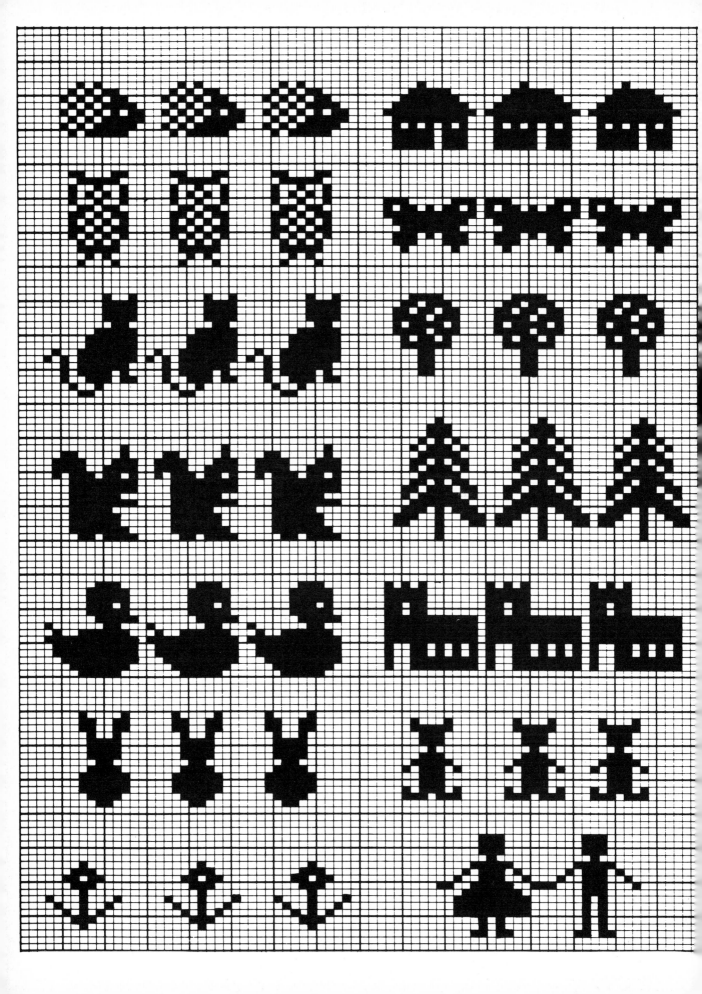

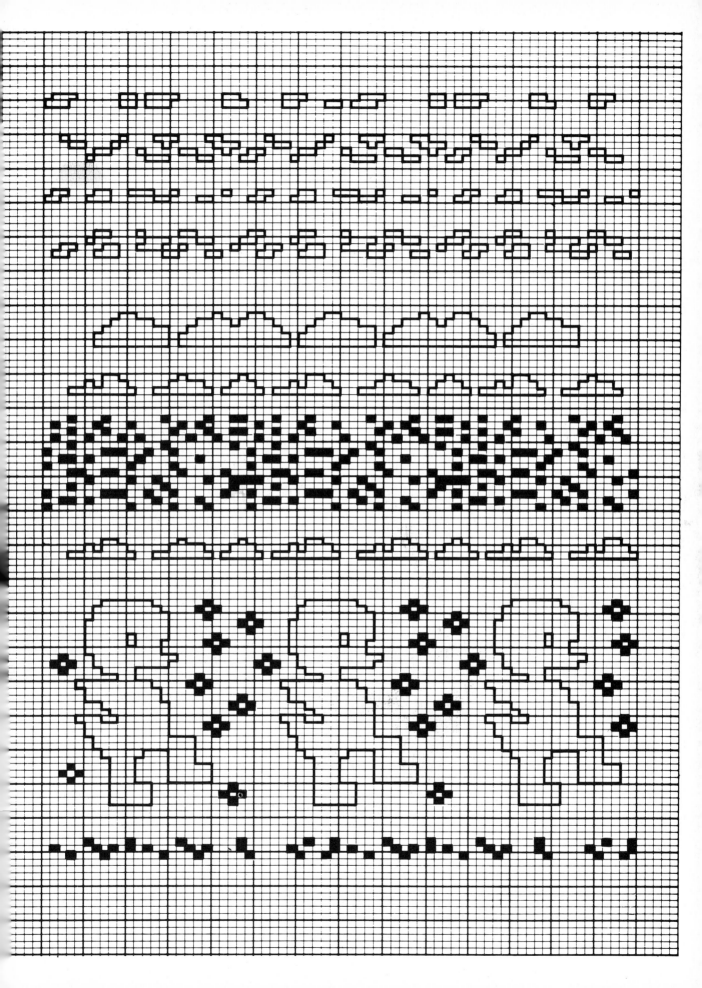

Main picture: Pheasant (page 99), Elephant (page 98), Clown (page 97), Pig on the Wall (page 67), Monkey on Branch (page 59) and Man in the Moon (page 102)

Small pictures: Improvised 'picture' designs using charts between pages 114 and 126.

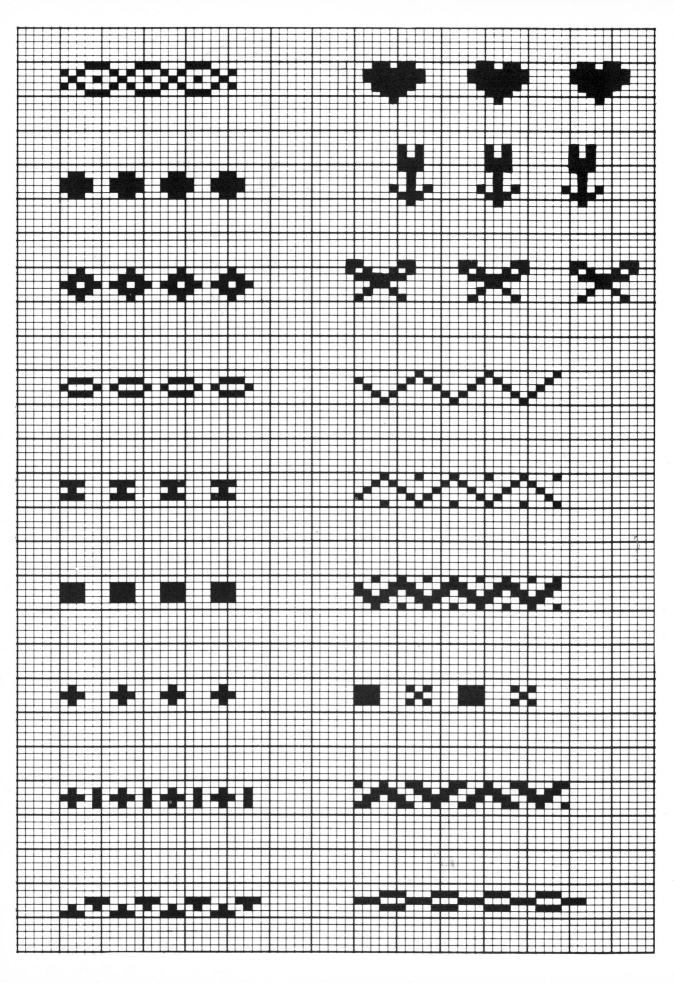

ACKNOWLEDGEMENTS

A book such as this is the result of a team effort. The designs not only have to be originated; they have to be tried out, corrected, and re-knitted. Then they have to be written out, carefully drawn and finally compiled into a book. Along the way, dozens of people become involved. There are, however, a few people who deserve a very special mention.

First of all, I would like to thank Penny Symonds who translated the designs into knitting patterns. Her technical expertise is unsurpassed. Penny is now passing on her skills to the lucky knitters of Crawley. Lena Kerry of Woolwork in Alton painstakingly read the manuscript and advised throughout. Her knowledge of the retail knitting trade has helped enormously.

Of several designers and illustrators who have helped, many of the original design concepts were drawn by Abigail Webster and Annabelle Smith. Zoe Gorham and Rupert Godsorton undertook the final artwork, a feat which required extraordinary precision and concentration.

Muriel Prince, my mother-in-law, was at the head of a band of knitters who made up the samples and whose dedication and feedback were of paramount importance. Thank you to everyone who patiently modelled the jumpers, whilst my husband, Brian, photographed them. He has spent many hours taking the photographs for this book. His comments and observations, his love and his strength, have kept me going when everything seemed to be an uphill struggle.

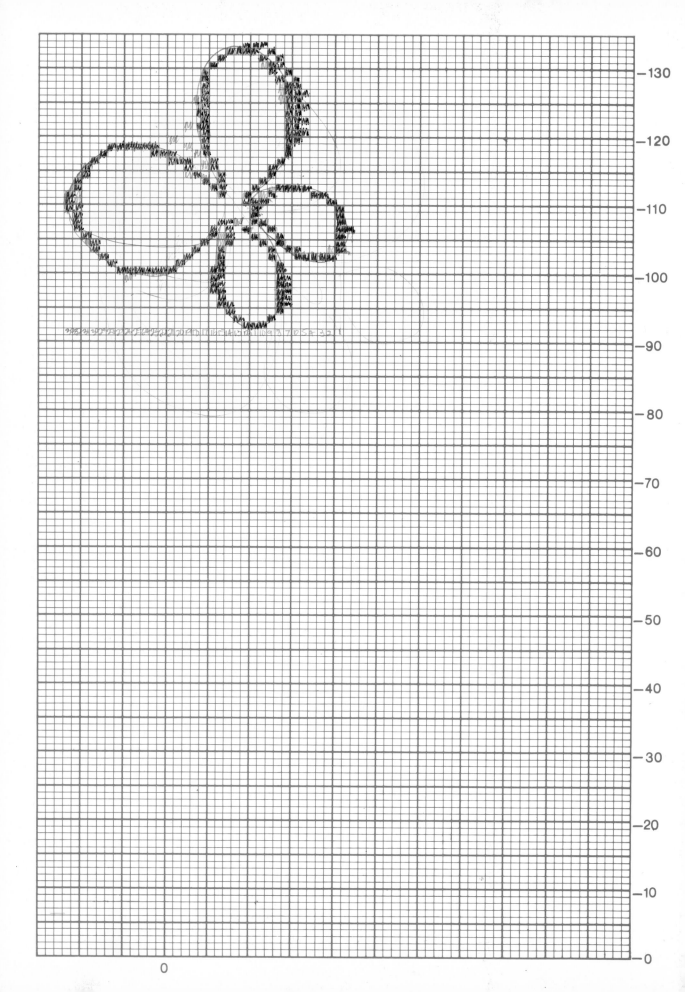